Jan's words here are like a literal gift to your heart and soul. Her masterful, luminous wisdom will not only inspire and encourage you to do the hard and holy work of digging deep into true community but will gently hand you the tools necessary to become a truly safe place for someone else's heart. Her life is a living, breathing example of friendship personified, and you'll close the pages of this book a better person because of it.

ANN VOSKAMP, *New York Times* bestselling author of *The Broken Way* and *One Thousand Gifts*

Spending a few hours with Jan Peterson is delicious! *Becoming Gertrude* is not only about spiritual friendship— it is a taste of the real thing. The most personal is the most universal, and this book is truth conveyed through personality. Read Jan's heart and then watch how she gently moves you forward in your faith journey. What a gift and what a delight!

R. PAUL STEVENS, professor emeritus of Marketplace Theology and Leadership at Regent College; chairman of the Institute for Marketplace Transformation

Jan Peterson's book *Becoming Gertrude* is a must-read. I find such inspiration in its life lessons that I walk away uplifted and motivated to care, accept, serve, offer hospitality, and encourage others in new ways. Her insights reveal how each of us is uniquely made and called to make a beautiful impact for the cause of love in tangible ways. I can't wait to live out this book's life-giving principles.

STASI ELDREDGE, *New York Times* bestselling author

I only recently met Jan, but her writing mirrors my experience of her: warm, direct, and insightful. We should all become Gertrude, we should all receive Gertrude, and we should all keep this book close by to read and read again.

ASHLEY CLEVELAND, Grammy-winning singer/songwriter and author

With warmth and wisdom, Janice Peterson beautifully reveals how loving others not only deepens our love for God but also brightens an often dark and lonely world. What a little gem this book is.

SUSAN MEISSNER, bestselling author of *As Bright as Heaven*

Like her welcoming friend, Gertrude, Jan Peterson welcomes her readers into a winsome, gentle conversation about the meaning and value of spiritual friendship. Through stories accumulated over decades of marriage and ministry alongside her pastor-husband, Eugene, Jan illustrates how each of us can create relationships that nurture our own soul and bless the world at the same time. I finished *Becoming Gertrude* with a reluctant sigh, because I wanted to hear more from this unpretentious and vibrant woman who possesses a true servant's heart.

KAY WARREN, cofounder of Saddleback Church

For sixty years, Jan Peterson has served Christ's church. But what stands out to me is the way she's done it. Instead of white-knuckling her way through, Jan has done this work with a gentle touch and an infectious joy. Her life is proof that the life of pastoral ministry can be a yoke that's easy and a burden that's light. While so many are familiar with Eugene's ministry, anyone who knows the Petersons knows that Jan has made Eugene's work possible all these years. She is one of those hidden figures that makes the Kingdom of God go. As I hold this book, I rejoice because the treasury of Jan Peterson's life is now available for generations to come. Now take and read.

DANIEL GROTHE, associate senior pastor of New Life Church, Colorado Springs, Colorado

Everyone needs a friend like Jan Peterson. She honors friendship as the sacrament it is, and in her personal and heartwarming story, *Becoming Gertrude*, Jan doesn't just celebrate this sacrament—she gently shares how to exercise our "caring muscles" in ways that truly matter. Jan's soulful and intentional approach to friendship is refreshing in this day of device-based interactions. She has inspired me, prompted me, and taught me more about the importance (and necessity!) of caring, acceptance, service, hospitality, and encouragement in our everyday, ordinary lives. The world needs more people like Jan and Eugene Peterson, who are day-to-day Christ followers in all they do—marriage, ministry, family, and friendship. *Becoming Gertrude* is a book that helps you become more like Jesus.

ANDREA SYVERSON, author of *Alter Girl: Walking Away from Religion into the Heart of Faith*

Having spent time in the Petersons' home, I can say that Jan lives what she writes. She exudes spiritual friendship with authenticity, passion, and grace. In our day of division, anger, and intolerance, we need people like her more than ever. Read this little gem slowly, soak it in, practice it faithfully, and live into it personally.

AARON STERN, lead pastor of Mill City Church, Fort Collins, Colorado

We all need spiritual friends—people who will walk beside us in our journey of faith, accepting us, helping us, encouraging us, and opening their lives to us. In *Becoming Gertrude*, Jan Peterson helps us see our need for such friendship through stories and experiences from her own life. May we, like Gertrude, show the love of God to others in real and tangible ways.

CHRISTINA FOX, author of *A Heart Set Free: A Journey to Hope through the Psalms of Lament* and *Closer Than a Sister: How Union with Christ Helps Friendships to Flourish*

Having experienced firsthand the hospitality of Jan Peterson, I know that what you're holding in your hand is not really a book; it is lived wisdom. Jan shares warmly and openly about her journey into discovering her identity and ministry through the gift of spiritual friends. If the early church grew exponentially largely because of their radical hospitality, Jan's words here will be more than advice for pastors' wives; they will be a pathway for recovering our great calling to share not only the gospel but also our lives with those around us.

GLENN PACKIAM, lead pastor of New Life Downtown, Colorado Springs, Colorado

Jan Peterson's reflections on spiritual friendship exude warmth and wisdom, just as she does. Her dedication to the practice of hospitality and faithful friendship over a lifetime is evident in every gracious word. *Becoming Gertrude* also invites us to explore our own unique calling to love and service and assures us we will never regret the journey. I am really grateful for this gem of a book.

> **JILL PHILLIPS**, singer/songwriter, Nashville, Tennessee

Jan Peterson is more than the woman behind the man behind *The Message*. At heart, she is a friend. These words on friendship are deep waters, but the best part is that they flow so naturally from her heart. And the words in these pages are winsome and true.

> **ALAN BRIGGS**, pastor, coach, consultant, and author of *Staying Is the New Going, Everyone's a Genius*, and *Guardrails*

In *Becoming Gertrude*, Jan Peterson makes friends with the truth that all are equal in the sight of the heavenly Father. In a culture addicted to leadership and hierarchy, this journey through the precious intricacies and intimacies of spiritual friendship is what our world needs. We all learn to accept the beautiful love of God, as experienced through the presence of the one sitting beside us.

> **LISA JOY SAMSON**, author of *Quaker Summer*, artist, mother, and friend

Spiritual friendship is an idea whose time has come again. In fact, it never went out of style. In our world where so many are desperate for genuine connection, Jan Peterson offers a refreshing call for us to go deeper with one another. I am thrilled to recommend Jan's warm account of how friendship shapes our faith.

DR. WINFIELD BEVINS, author and director of church planting at Asbury Seminary

There is much talk about spiritual friendships, but it has been going on for a long time . . . since at least the incident on the road to Emmaus! Jan has been on that road all her life—and we are invited to travel along with her, getting glimpses of what spiritual friendship actually looks and smells and tastes like when taken off its high-sounding pedestal. I was one of those who, at seminary, were taken under Jan's wing. That was twenty years ago. And we are still friends.

JULIE CANLIS, author of *A Theology of the Ordinary* and coproducer of *Godspeed*

Jan has written the kind of book that makes you feel as if you've had a refreshing, easy, honest conversation with her over coffee. It's a conversation that I desperately needed to have, one inspiring me to engage in the important work of caring and of receiving care. I know I will be visiting this book repeatedly when I need encouragement and clarity of vision from a spiritual friend.

PHAEDRA JEAN TAYLOR, writer and artist

BECOMING
Gertrude

HOW OUR FRIENDSHIPS
SHAPE OUR FAITH

JANICE PETERSON

NAVPRESS

*A NavPress resource published in alliance
with Tyndale House Publishers, Inc.*

NavPress is the publishing ministry of The Navigators, an international Christian organization and leader in personal spiritual development. NavPress is committed to helping people grow spiritually and enjoy lives of meaning and hope through personal and group resources that are biblically rooted, culturally relevant, and highly practical.

For more information, visit www.NavPress.com.

Becoming Gertrude: How Our Friendships Shape Our Faith

Copyright © 2018 by Janice Peterson. All rights reserved.

A NavPress resource published in alliance with Tyndale House Publishers, Inc.

NAVPRESS and the NAVPRESS logo are registered trademarks of NavPress, The Navigators, Colorado Springs, CO. *TYNDALE* is a registered trademark of Tyndale House Publishers, Inc. Absence of ® in connection with marks of NavPress or other parties does not indicate an absence of registration of those marks.

The Team: Don Pape, Publisher; Caitlyn Carlson, Acquisitions Editor; Elizabeth Symm, Copy Editor; Julie Chen, Designer

Cover illustration of filigree pattern copyright © Inna Sergi/Shutterstock. All rights reserved.

Cover illustrations of jars copyright © Tatyana Komtsyan/Shutterstock. All rights reserved.

Cover illustration of mint copyright © Ann Diidik/Shutterstock. All rights reserved.

Cover illustration of lemons copyright © Arsvik/Shutterstock. All rights reserved.

Cover photograph of paper texture copyright © katritch/iStockphoto. All rights reserved.

Author photograph copyright © by Miles Finch. Used by permission. All rights reserved.

Unless otherwise indicated, all Scripture quotations are taken from *THE MESSAGE*, copyright © 1993, 1994, 1995, 1996, 2000, 2001, 2002 by Eugene H. Peterson. Used by permission of NavPress. All rights reserved. Represented by Tyndale House Publishers, Inc. Scripture quotations marked NIV are taken from the Holy Bible, *New International Version,*® *NIV.*® Copyright © 1973, 1978, 1984, 2011 by Biblica, Inc.® Used by permission. All rights reserved worldwide. Scripture quotations marked RSV are taken from the Revised Standard Version of the Bible, copyright © 1952 [2nd edition, 1971] by the Division of Christian Education of the National Council of the Churches of Christ in the United States of America. Used by permission. All rights reserved.

Some of the anecdotal illustrations in this book are true to life and are included with the permission of the persons involved. All other illustrations are composites of real situations, and any resemblance to people living or dead is purely coincidental.

For information about special discounts for bulk purchases, please contact Tyndale House Publishers at csresponse@tyndale.com, or call 1-800-323-9400.

Cataloging-in-Publication Data is Available.

ISBN 978-1-63146-845-2

Printed in China

24	23	22	21	20	19	18
7	6	5	4	3	2	1

For Eugene

Contents

The Way of Spiritual Friendship

So here's what I want you to do, God helping you:
Take your everyday, ordinary life—your sleeping,
eating, going-to-work, and walking-around life—
and place it before God as an offering.

ROMANS 12:1

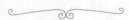

WHEN I WAS around thirteen years old, I discovered
the treasure of spiritual friendship through a woman
named Gertrude Floyd. Gertrude and her husband
were our back-door neighbors. On summertime
Saturday evenings, we usually had a cookout with the
Floyds in our backyard, around a picnic table laden

with meat from the barbeque pit my dad had built. There was always a lot of good food—hamburgers, salads, baked beans, delicious desserts—rich conversation, and laughter around that table.

As I entered into my teen years, I was growing in my heart and soul. I had recently been confirmed in the Presbyterian church and was involved in youth fellowship, where a lot of kind folks helped me center my life in the Lord. But a good deal of that growth came from just on the other side of our backyard fence. I often found myself walking through the back gate and knocking on Gertrude's screen door, where I was always received with a warm welcome and a "Come in—I'll get us some lemonade. You go on out to the porch."

I would freely talk to Gertrude about God and Jesus and things that were bothering me about school or one of my girlfriends—anything that might be on my mind. She always listened attentively and occasionally broke in with a question for clarification or to share a story that would help illuminate what I was talking about. She was always present. Always caring.

Those visits had a profound influence in my life. Even at thirteen, I was beginning to understand the kind of woman I wanted to be as I grew up: I wanted to be like Gertrude. Her loving friendship showed me how powerful it can be to live a life of being readily available to others—to listen, to care for them, to engage with their lives.

Several years ago, my husband, Eugene, was asked to speak to a conference of pastors and their wives in Colorado. After the first evening of worship and introductions, several women came up to me and asked if I would be willing to meet with them after breakfast each morning, the hour before the general session. The next morning, we sat in chairs around the open fireplace and talked about where we served with our husbands and what kinds of things we were wrestling with. Those were good hours together. Most of the women contributed in some way, and the honesty and wisdom that emerged through the conversations were deeply meaningful. The gathering would not have been as rich if even one of them had not come. As I listened to the women around me, I felt in my heart a quickening, a desire to listen more and speak into their lives when it seemed appropriate. I saw in that group the same kindness and relationship I'd seen in Gertrude—the desire to encourage, to share wisdom, not from a compelling need to speak or prove ourselves, but to care and love well the others around us.

I recently received a letter from the husband of one of these women. He told me how helpful those long-ago conversations continue to be to his wife. That is the value of profound friendship, of investing deeply in the lives of others: Our words and actions have an impact beyond what we can ever fully see.

Dorothy Day, cofounder of the Catholic Worker movement, said:

> We cannot love God unless we love each other, and to love we must know each other. We know Him in the breaking of bread, and we know each other in the breaking of bread, and we are not alone any more. Heaven is a banquet and life is a banquet, too, even with a crust, where there is companionship.

> We have all known the long loneliness and
> we have learned that the only solution is love
> and that love comes with community.[1]

I would call that community, those dear people who show us the love of God, "spiritual friendship."

What do I mean by "spiritual friendship"? Well, let me tell you a story. A young woman once asked me if I would be her spiritual mentor. It was the first time in my life anyone had asked me that. I sat there for a few seconds before replying, "I don't think I can do that, Jean. But what I can do is be a spiritual friend with you. If that sounds okay to you, I'd love doing that. I always think of a mentor as someone knowing more than the other person and being 'above' them. I think you and I could have some good sharing in our conversations that would encourage each of us— I would see our time as mutually beneficial. I probably have more life experiences to share, but you also have life to share with me, even though you are younger than me. This is a back-and-forth sharing we can do together."

Being in this kind of friendship means that someone cares about me and is willing to listen attentively—and I do the same for them. These kinds of friends are precious; they are not people who only take or who choose to keep me at arm's length. No, a spiritual friend chooses to love in tangible ways and wants me to grow in the things of God.

The reason I think it's important to distinguish spiritual friendship from the idea we know as "mentoring" is that spiritual friendship isn't any kind of hierarchy—it's not one person as the "expert" and the other as the "learner." Spiritual friendship is learning to see the worth God has placed in each person and appreciating the gifts individuals have to offer. It's being willing to share when you need to share and learn when you need to learn. It's caring for the well-being of the other person, and letting her care for you as well. Giving and receiving. Walking side by side through different seasons of life. We are all richer for understanding not only what we have to offer the people in our lives, but understanding what they have to offer, as well.

In my richest friendships, I've made intentional decisions to love the other person well. I've made myself available so they know I'm there to listen. I ask them questions that help me understand what they're feeling. It takes time and creativity, but the spiritual value and growth that come through these relationships are so important. We all need these kinds of spiritual friendships to weather both the good and the bad of life—to encourage others forward in their faith and to find encouragement ourselves.

And we women so often find ourselves in life situations or seasons in which we need encouragement, don't we? One thing that came up several times as I talked with pastors' wives was how much they needed someone to talk to when they were struggling with something or someone in the church. Being a pastor's wife can be very isolating. One can feel very alone. And that goes for so many of us, no matter what our role. Life itself can feel isolating. How many of us feel lonely even when we are surrounded by people? Perhaps you are home with small children and wondering when you will get to have a grown-up conversation. Perhaps you feel you are running ragged to-and-fro from work and feel too tired to find friends after a long day. Perhaps you simply struggle to connect with the people around you, and you wonder if anyone will ever see you for who you are.

I've felt that way myself, especially in the early days of our pastorate. Eugene was off tending to the people in our congregation, and I was at home raising young children. It was hard to find the time or energy to really get to know someone, or to be known. Which is a discouraging place to be, particularly as a follower of Jesus.

Relationship in the body of Christ is where we grow best. Of course, we must pursue our relationship with God day in and day out as well: having a quiet time in the morning, an intentional time with God, and participating in regular worship. But community is vital for spiritual growth; our friends can challenge us, sharpen us, and restore us in unique and powerful ways. We experience his presence with others just as much as when we're alone in prayer with him. In our friendships, we are pointed to him again and again, we are refined, and we are encouraged, even when we feel like we are failing. But when we feel isolated, we feel stuck. And I don't want to downplay the struggles of being in that place. I don't want to make it sound like there's some magical, simple solution to your isolation. It's not easy to build spiritual friendships. It's not easy to invest in the lives of those around you in a way that grows both of you more in Christ. But I can promise you this: It is absolutely worth it. The hard work you do now to carve out time, to push through weariness and discouragement, will enrich your life and your faith in ways you can't imagine. We need each other. It's just part of how we were meant to be.

I had to make that choice to reach out and find spiritual friends. Those early isolating days were a significant season in my life. I was wrestling with a fundamental question: Just who is this person Jan Peterson? And so, in the midst of all the busyness of that time, I made the decision to pursue help. I didn't know I was looking for spiritual friendship, but that's what I needed. And one person who became a spiritual friend to me in that time was Ray.

Eugene and I had first met Ray when he served in our town as a Roman Catholic priest. This was around the time of Vatican II, when both Catholics and Protestants were encouraged to break down the walls that had been erected in Luther's day. Eventually, Ray wrote to the Vatican, asking to be relieved of his priesthood; he became a Lutheran pastor and married one of the ex-nuns he had worked with in our town. They served in a Lutheran church west of our town, close to Washington, DC.

Our family was on vacation when I wrote to Ray, asking for advice. Eugene had invited a family in our church to come stay with us in Montana. He had been counseling them in their troubled marriage and thought it might help them to get away together and spend time with us. Frankly, I was kind of mad. No, more than mad—I was having to do on our vacation what I do the other eleven months of the year at home! More cooking and tending to the needs of others when I needed a change from all that. I'm not sure what I expected of Ray, but I just needed to talk to someone I respected and get my frustrations out in the open.

Eugene has always encouraged me in what I do and appreciated the things I do for others, but I was in need now of an outside confidant—someone who could see things more simply without getting distracted with all the other stuff a spouse might know. Roman Catholic priests are trained to listen and give good guidance, which is why Ray seemed like the right person for me to call on. I really thought he would make a suggestion of someone in our town. He said he didn't know of anyone to suggest but that I could come and see him. So that is what I did.

When I drove the two hours to see Ray that initial time, we first caught up with each other's lives, and then he asked me to tell him again why I was so frustrated with my dear husband. Quite practically, he suggested that I talk to Eugene and express to him that I was in need of a vacation as much as he was. He was helping me see what was beneath my frustration: that as a pastor's wife, I was in ministry as much as my husband was, and Eugene and I needed to understand our common ground. But then Ray pushed me a step further. As a true spiritual friend,

he saw that my angst was also connected to identity—
to that question of who I was and what my purpose
was, particularly in this season of life. He suggested
that I write down for him what I saw as my gifts and
how I was using them. The next month, when I went
back and read my list aloud to him, we talked about
the expressions of my gifts.

Ray wasn't the only person who taught me about
spiritual friendship during that time. In fact, because
of Ray, I learned that our spiritual friends can play
different roles in our lives. Ray exhibited spiritual
friendship in some of the big things in my life.

My new companion, Clare, was a friend to me
in the ordinary things of life—all those things that
have to be repeated over and over, day by day. I like
how writer Kathleen Norris phrased it in her book
title *The Quotidian Mysteries: Laundry, Liturgy and
"Women's Work."* Clare and I knew that language well.
Caring for a home and family can often be boring,
repetitive work. But we talked about how we could
see all of this work as being offered up to God. She
and I met weekly to talk and pray with each other

about how we could live the ordinary things of life to the glory of God.

While our friendship was focused on those everyday rhythms, we found that God led us into deeper and even more powerful things. We learned to trust each other with the harder questions and conversations because we knew we could trust each other in the ordinary things. For example, Clare was the daughter of a Lutheran pastor, so she knew what my life as a pastor's wife was like. I was able to share what I was going through and learn from her wisdom and experience as well.

Sometimes, Clare and I would go to the Catholic church in her neighborhood and pray together the stations of the cross on a circular path in the garden. We learned that Mary, the mother of Jesus, had prayed *fiat mihi*—"be it done unto me"—and Mary's prayer became an important part of what we were doing and talking about together. When Eugene and I moved out of the state, Clare and I gave each other a simple necklace with *Fiat Mihi* embossed on the front and *F.F.* on the back—Faithful Friendship.

As a young person, I always felt that I compartmentalized my Christianity. It was easy to see how I was supposed to follow God in the traditional rhythms of church and reading the Bible but harder to understand what it looked like in my everyday life. It always bothered me that my Christianity didn't permeate all areas of my life. I was a Christian, but that didn't always come out in all my normal, day-to-day activities. Having friends like Clare and Ray helped me integrate it into all aspects of my days—especially the ordinariness of life, where Christ is in my daily living.

In both the big and small things of life, I learned and grew more by having a friend who was processing things with me. That's why spiritual friendship is so important. God created us for community, not for living this life in Christ by ourselves.

Choosing to see friendships as an integral part of my faith brought me into a new way of living. Once a month, I would drive over to see Ray and have rich conversations with him, and every week, Clare and I met to encourage each other to live to God's honor and glory in the common, daily ordinariness of life.

Up to that point, I had lived my Christian life compartmentally. Now, my faith was feeling more whole, more integrated, as a big part of who I was as a child of God—the person I was allowing God to shape.

When Eugene and I moved to Regent College in Vancouver, Canada, things got reversed—after being fed and growing through the investment of people like Ray and Clare, I was suddenly equipped to do the same for others, and God brought all sorts of opportunities for me to do so. That's the thing about growing spiritually—it always pushes us into new places and new experiences, and we get to pass along what we've learned.

If we are intentional in our friendships, those people can help us see how God is working in our lives. Good friends challenge us in the areas where we are weak and encourage us forward. Spiritual friendship takes us to a depth of relationship that enriches us both—it's hard to stay shallow when we decide to be honest about our relationship with God and what he is teaching us. When we invest in those sorts of friendships, every part of our lives becomes richer, because we are allowing God to speak into all of our experiences.

And of course, spiritual friendships are not a one-way path of growth. As we allow people to build into us, we are enabled and strengthened to build into others. In healthy friendships, we care deeply for our friends, seeking to hold them up in their weak places. We learn to lovingly accept each person's heart and gifts. We develop the desire to serve those around us. We reach out in hospitality, providing a safe and warm space for our friends to be with us. And above all, we learn to live in the rhythm of encouragement, speaking life and hope often. I have found these five elements of spiritual friendship—caring, accepting, serving, offering hospitality, and encouraging others—woven throughout my life and relationships. Each of these things overlaps and flows through the others, creating a strong cord of friendship that cannot be broken.

As you and I step forward into this book, I hope I can share a little of what I've learned so that you may both receive and give to others in rich relationship.

I'm not here as a teacher or to tell people how to live. Everybody's got to do that on their own before God. I'm here as a friend. Let's walk together and uncover the beauty of spiritual friendship.

REFLECTIONS ON

Spiritual Friendship

1. What do you think about what Jan describes as the difference between a mentor and a spiritual friend? Who has been a spiritual friend to you?

2. What barriers do you face to building rich spiritual friendships?

3. What are you currently wrestling with that would benefit from someone speaking into your life? Who do you know (even if you don't know them well!) who could provide insight and help?

4. Who in your life can you reach out to and invest in? How has God equipped you to do that?

5. Jan shares five elements of spiritual friendship that have particularly impacted her life: caring, accepting, serving, offering hospitality, and encouraging others. Which of these is hardest for you? Which of these comes easily to you?

CHAPTER 1

CARING

Choosing to See Others

. . . and place it before God as an offering.

ROMANS 12:1

$\sim\!\!\sim\!\!\sim$

𝓗OW DO WE BECOME caring people? When I pondered that question, one word came to my mind: *practice*. We all start out self-centered—me, me, me. In order to develop a caring spirit, we need to become intentionally aware of the needs of others. As we begin to see the needs all around us, and make it our mission to address those needs, caring for others gets worked into the fabric of our lives.

1

Becoming Gertrude

Our first practice of caring often comes through the home we grew up in. All of us are selfish as little people. Our wants are our world. And so perhaps a parent, an older sibling, or a grandparent identified and corrected our behavior time and time again, pointing out when we were being uncaring and coaching us toward behavior that showed love for others.

Perhaps we saw a caring spirit modeled by those closest to us in our growing-up years, as I saw in my visits with Gertrude, visit after visit. My parents also showed me what it looked like to care for other people—my father particularly. And I just soaked that in. Part of growing our caring muscles, practicing how to care for someone else, is paying attention to who is doing it well around us.

If you didn't grow up in an environment where caring was normal, I'm so sorry. My heart aches for the young people I see in our community who are trying to live in the midst of painful circumstances. More and more families are broken, and more and more kids are growing up in difficult situations. But just because you grew up in a hard home doesn't mean you can't develop rich spiritual friendships. You, too, can exercise your caring muscles. Observe someone you admire. Find someone who could sit with you and talk about what caring for people looks like. We become like those we spend the most time with. So choose to spend time with people who are caring.

But at some point, simply seeing caring in action or being told to do it isn't enough. We have to choose to look outside ourselves. We have to choose to see the hurting people in our community—or right next door. And in our friendships, we have to choose to say, "You first." What does that mean? Well, it means being slow to speak and quick to listen. What does the person in front of you need? Are you willing to make yourself uncomfortable and even inconvenienced to step into those needs with them? Maybe it's simply listening and offering words of love and encouragement, or maybe it's taking the time to help them move or to watch their kids or to make them a meal. Jesus said, "Do to others as you would have them do to you."[2] And "love one another; for love is of God."[3] This others-focused life is the life God wants us to live—a life of not overlooking the needs around us but of choosing to see and deciding to care.

But—and this is important—sometimes in all that caring for others, we need to learn how to care for ourselves as well. This is different from a selfish, me-first attitude; instead, it's being aware enough to not overdo it, to take a deep breath and maybe seek out a spiritual elder or soul friend to talk to if your caring gets off-balance. We cannot care well for others if we are burned out and exhausted. We are not supposed to set our needs aside completely. We must understand when we hit our limit and when our caring for others becomes unhelpful because we're doing it from a completely empty place. And, like all aspects of spiritual friendship, this is when we need to be humble enough to receive. Let your friends care for you. Let them help you when you are in need of support, whether emotional or physical or spiritual. And as you are filled, pass the gift along.

It's appropriate that we should look at this idea of caring first, because if we do not care for others, the foundation of spiritual friendship is nonexistent. We cannot accept, serve, show hospitality, or encourage others without first caring for them.

As we seek to care for others, we can easily limit ourselves to wherever we feel most comfortable. But to truly develop a caring spirit in our spiritual friendships, we need to be intentional, to care for people in all aspects of our lives. We can't simply choose to care for those who are easy to care about. It's like Jesus said in Luke 6:32-33 (NIV), "If you love those who love you, what credit is that to you? . . . And if you do good to those who are good to you, what credit is that to you?" We all like to care for people who are easy to love. But caring needs to go beyond that to people who are hard to love, whether because of personality differences or relational struggles or simply the fact that they're strangers.

As we unpack this component of caring in spiritual friendship, we need to pay attention to every single aspect: caring for the larger world, caring for the needy in our communities, and caring for the people we're in regular relationship with. Keeping in mind this larger vision of caring will develop a compassion and sensitivity to see each and every person as God sees them, and it will help us know how best to reach out to them with care. In spiritual friendship, we need to trust God's leading for how to best care for the people he's placed in our lives. Learning to care in every aspect of our lives will help us do that.

CARING FOR THE WORLD

Caring for the larger world involves awareness, compassion, and sacrifice. We need to develop hearts that are aware of what God is doing, where people in the world are being treated unfairly or hurting, and what we can do about it. Caring always involves action. It's not just a feeling.

For me, caring in this way first emerged in the '60s, as I was faced with the issues of peace and racial justice. But as I saw the racial tensions around me and I became more and more aware of the unjust ways African Americans were treated, I knew that caring meant I needed to get involved. I joined our county's

Fair Housing Committee to advocate for what I knew was right.

When my neighbor across the street learned of my involvement, he wasn't very happy. He was a member of St. Margaret's Catholic Church in Bel Air and was apparently getting his ears full from the priests about the injustice of unfair housing. He said to me one day, "You people who don't own your own houses can talk this way because you don't have any investment in a house. You have nothing to lose. We do. If a black family were to move into our neighborhood, our property value would go way down."

As he criticized me, I realized that a lot more was at stake than just a good idea about equality for all. What I believed couldn't just stay an idea. Standing up for what was right was going to take action. I needed to actively care for people who were being treated unjustly.

I stayed on the Fair Housing Committee.

The Catholics were being very outspoken about the issue of fair housing, so one day I asked Eugene why he didn't preach about fair housing and other civil rights issues. He said, "I believe if I preach biblically and show people the gospel as lived out that they'll 'get' it. That they will see and grow into this from who they are learning to be and not by having it imposed on them from the outside." I respected that. We each cared for others, but our approaches were different—his was preaching the gospel and encouraging people toward heart change, and mine was getting more actively involved in specific issues.

In the places and ways we care for the larger world around us, change doesn't take place overnight. Growth is slow. I have learned that firsthand over the years. I know that the end results are more solid and true if change emerges out of God's work in our hearts as he shows us how to care for the people around us. If I just do what someone tells me to do out of my Christian duty, my care for others doesn't get embedded as deeply in my heart. If my character and conscience are informed, my care for others is more solid, more real, and more true.

As we work out our "care muscles," we might be surprised by how our hearts expand to reach out further to the world around us. This was certainly true for me. Around the same time that I started working for fair housing, I began reading about world hunger. The denomination was speaking up about it, and the more I learned, the more I wanted to learn and figure out what I could do. I couldn't solve world hunger, but I could learn to see the needs of others and understand the impact of how we live here in America. I could do something tangible to remind myself of the needs around the world and help others see them as well. That's the thing about developing a heart to care for the world: You don't have to do big things. You can simply do small things right where you are.

The concern about world hunger was in the air at that time. It wasn't just something I was wrestling with—it was on the minds and hearts of people who were conscientious about the world around them. Choosing to be a part of that conversation was another way of practicing caring; I was observing the caring people around me and what they were paying attention to, and that helped me choose to pay attention to the struggles in the world around me.

Being observant like this also sensitizes you to people around you who are less fortunate. It makes you aware of what other people are going through. Having that spirit within you helps you notice more and more and see things that are not the way they should be.

As I learned more about world hunger, I decided that a practical way for me to understand the struggles of others more deeply was to change how I cooked and ate. I got books out of the library. I bought the *More-with-Less Cookbook* by Doris Janzen Longacre. Then I came across Frances Moore Lappé's work in eating less or no meat using her study of complementary proteins in her *Diet for a Small Planet*, and I read its companion book, *Recipes for a Small Planet*, by Ellen Buchman Ewald. We started eating fewer meat-based meals and more complementary protein dishes. Using food resources differently seemed like a simple and sensible way to remind myself of the hunger of others in my everyday life.

After getting into the rhythm of cooking and eating this way, I wanted to share what I had learned and get other people engaged with the hunger issues in our world and how our eating habits could make a positive difference for others. So I put together kitchen labs for any women in our church who might be interested. Then, at the beginning of Lent, I put together a program after our Lenten dinner to talk about what we as a congregation could do to help alleviate some of the magnitude of suffering that other countries were facing. I showed a film during the program to help provide broader perspective; it was mostly on multinational corporations and how we Americans were using much more of the world's resources than any other nation per capita.

It was at this point that I was once again faced with the choice to evaluate my commitment to care for those facing injustice and pain in the world around me. (I'm not saying everyone is going to be led to care for the same things—but this is where I had been drawn to.) A man in our church who was (and still is) a good friend was fairly offended by the point made in the film—because he worked for a multinational company. Ouch! Here I was again, facing pushback for where God was leading me in caring for others, just as I'd experienced with my stance on fair housing. More soul-searching. More prayer. More commitment than I had bargained on. (After all, I'm just a sweet southern belle!) But my heart and spirit said I must share about the poverty and injustice in the world.

We're not necessarily going to change the world with our decisions. I knew that. But if we're faithful to act and engage, maybe our hearts and commitments will follow—and maybe those around us will be encouraged to care more deeply in turn.

We had a good friend visit us as I was engaging with this conversation about world hunger. He traveled a lot with an organization that worked with helping people. And this friend of ours loved meat! He always ordered steak when eating out in a restaurant because "you can't do much to hurt steak." I was having a meatless meal the night he was with us, so I told him a little apologetically what I was doing. "You're not going to make much impact on world hunger around your dining-room table!" he said.

"I know," I told him, "but it might change me so

that I'm more aware, more conscious of others with much less than I have." And I know it has. And I hope it changed some of the families in our church as well, and—who knows?—their children, too.

CARING FOR THE NEEDY

Jesus tells us to care for others. We live very selfishly as a culture. Choosing to see what others are going through, caring for them in the midst of what they're dealing with, helps us get outside of our selfish mindsets and understand what other people need. We need to choose to be aware. Caring for others doesn't mean looking down on them. But it does mean entering into their world, coming alongside them, showing them compassion and respect. While caring for the larger world is a good start, we can put our commitment into even more direct action by caring for the needy in our communities.

The women from our church, along with people from other churches in the county, had a clothing center where needy folks could come and buy clothing.

Yes, *buy*. A quarter for a pair of kids' jeans, fifteen cents for a shirt. A quarter for a pair of shoes, etc. Being able to buy something ourselves, no matter how small the cost, helps us find self-respect and dignity, even in financially hard situations. Now, if someone really wanted something but didn't have any more money, we'd laugh and say something like "I can see you can't live without that dress. So just take it. And enjoy wearing it because the color is great for you."

I currently volunteer at our local food bank and enjoy that so much. I need to volunteer working with those less fortunate than myself. When you live in suburbia with all your neighbors financially on par with you, you need to be reminded that some people have harder lives and struggle to make ends meet.

In the early years of our marriage, I sometimes felt like I was the "other." Eugene and I were right down near the poverty level. Our home was provided for us by the church, so our salary wasn't on par with our neighbors'. But I eventually realized that we were making less each year because we weren't getting a cost-of-living increase. I was married to a pastor who wasn't making that much anyway—and still, for years, he wouldn't accept a raise in salary when the financial committee suggested it because he "just wanted the church to get on its feet" financially.

It was during these times of need that others reached out and showed me what caring truly looks like. I remember walking down the aisles of the grocery store one summer day, trying to figure out what I could possibly buy for supper that night. But cooking everything from scratch helped. No prepared foods. It was right after that summer day that a woman in our church started bringing us produce from her wonderful garden. A lifesaver! She also loved our children and bought them a pony for them to ride at her place.

In the midst of all of our caring for others, loving and serving a church congregation and stretched thin financially, someone cared for us.

We were a one-car family at that time, so Eugene and I had to plan ahead for when I could use the car for grocery shopping. One day, friends from our former church in New York called us up and told us they had a Renault that the husband had been using to drive to the train station for his daily commute into the city. He wouldn't be needing the car any longer—would we have use for it?

Would we? We drove up the next week to pick up our little car. But at the same time our friends cared so generously and specifically for our needs, I remember feeling like a charity case. As someone born at the end of the Great Depression, I had never been given much in life and I never really expected anything, much less a car. But I had to push down my pride. We were not within walking distance of anything except our church, which was a quarter mile away. This had been a cornfield one-and-a-half miles from the town of Bel Air, our little colonial town. With a second car, Eugene and I didn't have to jostle the use of a vehicle.

I had to push down my pride a number of times. Parishioners who were moving to Florida had a freezer they weren't taking with them and wondered if we might like to have it. Someone also gave me blankets and sheets they weren't using. I put them to good use on my daughter's twin beds. A number of other gifts came along the way.

I was grateful for the generosity of our friends. I was glad I learned to push down my pride and allowed our friends to show me what unselfish caring looked like.

Caring for the needy makes me more sensitive to what all the people around me are going through. It helps me sense when someone in my life is struggling, and it helps me have the awareness to speak kindly and carefully into a friend's life when I understand that they may be going through all sorts of things I can't see.

CARING FOR THE PERSON IN FRONT OF ME

Of course, caring for others is perhaps found in its most important form in our everyday relationships. Reaching out to the larger world and serving the needy among us are both ways to develop a caring heart, but we are pushed into more specific and sacrificial forms of caring for others, and spiritual friendship is most fully evidenced, when we care for the person right in front of us—the woman at church, the friend going through a hard time in her marriage, the coworker or next-door neighbor.

As with so many things in life, I learned this for myself in an unexpected way. When we first moved into our "house church," I wanted a garden—but I was much too busy tending to babies and keeping the church clean and picked up in case someone from the congregation showed up (and my house "showed up" what kind of a housewife I really was). So I postponed having a vegetable garden. I planted a few flowers; we had the yard landscaped (with the help of a former parishioner from our New York church, who was also a good friend). And, because I love having flowers in my house, I had Eugene dig one flower bed toward the back of our half-acre lot, close to where our back-door neighbors', Mike and Alma's, joined ours. One morning, when I looked out my back window, I saw Mike at my flower bed, just looking at it. I walked out and greeted him, and he said, "Humpf. I grow food." I smiled at him and said, "That's nice."

The children and I would see him in his vegetable

garden, working under his spotlight in the evenings. We even started referring to him as "Farmer McGregor." When I told him what the children were calling him, he was confused. He had never heard of Farmer McGregor. I said, "Peter Rabbit, you know?" He had never heard of Peter Rabbit! This man was totally deprived. I wondered what his home life had been like growing up.

He and Alma had no children, which meant he hadn't had that second chance to learn of Peter Rabbit and Farmer McGregor. So the next opportunity I had, I delivered the large-print picture book of *Peter Rabbit* for Mike to read. I would have loved to watch this chemist from Edgewood Chemical Biological Center sitting in his living room and reading about the farmer chasing Peter Rabbit out of his vegetable garden.

As the children got a little older and became more independent, I asked Eugene to rent a rototiller and dig a garden for me to grow vegetables. As a chemist, Mike knew what chemicals do to our bodies, which is why he grew all of his vegetables organically. He started teaching me what not to do and what to do, like mulching a garden so you didn't have to hoe or weed. I had a good farmer friend, Jeffrey, in lower Pennsylvania who gave me truckloads of sour and rotting hay for mulch. As Jeffrey and I pitched the hay off the truck, we got a bonus as well (if you could call it that). A black racer snake slithered out of the hay pile. Now, snakes are one creature I had always felt we could do without. I still do. But Mike told me that the snake would take care of any mice that might be around. So we let him be.

I planted my seeds and seed potatoes and seedlings in rows, laid newspaper down over the ground, and tossed the hay over the newspaper. I loved my new garden. The potatoes were especially nice—I could pick them by just lifting the newspaper up and taking the small new potatoes off their runners without disturbing the whole plant.

One morning at breakfast, I saw something strange in my vegetable garden. I went outside and started laughing. Mike had "planted" flowers for me. They were plastic. His joke was a sweet sign of friendship.

He had stepped out of his normal routine and cared for his neighbor by teaching me almost all that I know about organic gardening—and now he was showing me that he was on my side by "planting" flowers for me! Because of Mike, I enjoyed learning all the how-tos and planting a huge variety of vegetables—carrots, broccoli, turnips, onions, tomatoes, garlic, sweet potatoes, white potatoes, okra, corn, kohlrabi, and squash. Each year I would try more and different ones. Our summer season wasn't quite long enough for me to try watermelons, although Mike did and shared them with our children.

I'd never before had anybody do what Mike did for me. There he was, a chemist with no children, but he chose to get involved in my life. I learned how much it means to have someone choose to see my needs and address them. It was such a surprise—we hardly knew each other! He had no reason to help me. But he chose to take time out of his day, see what I needed, and reach out to help. That's caring well for the person in front of you. Like him, I want to be a caring person and extend myself to others.

Many years back, I had a young friend, a girl from our neighborhood. I first noticed her as Eugene and I walked the quarter mile from house to church, church to house; we would often see this young woman riding her bicycle, going really fast and pounding away. We knew that she lived down the street, and we began to learn that she had some struggles. One day, a neighbor called Eugene up and told us the young lady was in the psych ward—and that it was her birthday. Could he go visit her?

When Eugene visited that day, she told him that she was growing tomato plants in her closet from seed (she lived in the woods and couldn't plant anything there), and Eugene told her she was welcome to use our yard. She came into our backyard, and I went out there and helped her grow things. We'd go play in the snow together in the winter, and other times, we'd go to the park and swing on the swings. I tried one day to say something about God to her, and I could tell I'd better not say anything any more. She didn't have any of that in her life. I was going to pray for her—that would be enough for now.

This young woman needed love and attention. Her parents struggled to understand what she was going through, so I had the opportunity to show her love and remind her of her worth. That little girl finished school, went to a wonderful university, and was going to become a doctor. She dropped out after two years, but then she got her PhD and finished her degree to become a doctor. It's amazing what she has done.

I couldn't help but care for her when she was in a vulnerable season. She was right there. Caring is choosing to see someone. Choosing to be with them right where they are. Choosing to connect with them and listen to what they need. Caring for someone isn't about you—it's about the other person.

A BALANCING ACT

Part of being a good spiritual friend is caring deeply—in emotion and through actions—for the people around us. But being a caring person also requires care for ourselves. I see so many people not balancing their lives well, overextending themselves. We can't effectively care for others if we're tired, burned out, emotionally drained—if we're not taking care of ourselves.

I certainly dealt with this. Being a pastor's wife brings with it a lot of demands. How do we keep our lives in balance? How do we keep ourselves healthy and well? In a life of ministry and caring for others, we need to have a center of gravity, a strong sense of self, a centering to keep ourselves sane and well. Even at this time in our lives, when Eugene and I are no longer working out of a church or school and have no secretary, no office with assistants, or even volunteers to recruit, we find that balance hard. These days, I get tired easily. And God has to take care of me outside myself.

When we feel overwhelmed, we need outside help. Sometimes it is in those periods in our lives (and probably before that happens) that we need a spiritual friend we can reach out to and they to us. We can talk it out; lay out our thoughts, problems, and ideas before a spiritual friend; and let them give us ideas to think about and ask good questions for us to think and pray and act upon. A good listener can make all the difference in the world as we struggle with issues that are unsettling to and in us. But a spiritual friend doesn't tell us what to do. They make suggestions and help to clarify what we are experiencing. Spiritual friendship is not problem-solving as such. It is about being in their presence and listening to them, caring about them.

As spiritual friends reach out in care to us, we are equipped to do that to others—to see someone else struggling in turn, whether in our world, our community, or next door. We can show care and love to someone else and help them find a place of balance and perspective through how we care for them in spiritual friendship.

Caring

1. Who in your life exhibits a caring spirit? What do you learn from observing them?

2. What issues in the world do you find yourself caring about? What small things can you do to put that care into action?

3. Where do you see needs in your local community? How can you care in action for those people?

4. Who in your everyday life needs intentional care? How can you reach out to them?

5. Do you struggle with overextending yourself in caring for others? Who can you lean on more to offer help and wisdom?

CHAPTER 2

ACCEPTANCE

Receiving What Is Offered

Embracing what God does for you is the best
thing you can do for him. Don't become so well-
adjusted to your culture that you fit into it without
even thinking. Instead, fix your attention on God.
You'll be changed from the inside out.

ROMANS 12:2

W̶HAT DOES IT really mean to accept someone in
friendship? In our current age, *acceptance* and *toler-
ance* are hard words. We find it difficult to understand those who disagree with us. We struggle to

accept those who are different from us. But when I think about acceptance in spiritual friendship, I like to set all of that baggage aside. As the dictionary says, acceptance is simply the action of consenting to receive or undertake something offered. So what are those around us offering in friendship? And are we willing to receive the gifts and love that are being offered? Are we willing to accept people as God made them?

A spiritual friend is someone you enjoy being with, but you may not always find the friendship simple or straightforward. The important thing is that you're able to spend time and go deep with that person, and you learn to appreciate each other's differences. The differences between us and others are valuable and help us have more profound perspectives on our own lives. My friend Jean and I are different in so many ways. I was a Protestant pastor's wife; Jean was Roman Catholic and planned on being a nun. She traveled all around the world to find her niche. But accepting the differences made our friendship so much richer. I really respected and admired her, particularly in how she was taking deliberate steps to serve in the best way she could.

Sometimes I've had friendships with people who are going through a difficult time in their marriage, and even having those marriages come to an end. But I come alongside them, listen to them, and provide a solid friendship for them that they can depend on, no matter what they're going through. Acceptance is not running away when things get hard. It's not being friends only when it's easy. It's choosing to invest and love no matter the circumstance.

ACCEPTING OTHERS

I am what you might call a "classic" extrovert. I like people—a lot. I like to be with people. I need socialization. And so, as a people person, I tend to accept and like people at face value. But even in my experience as an extrovert, I've found that there are three levels of accepting others, and it's important to discern which is which in our lives.

Some people, the ones in the first level, are easy

to accept and love, because we're in similar seasons of life and we "get" each other. In these friendships, acceptance is often about more superficial things— opinions about politics, or simply a struggle connecting because of different schedules. We must learn to navigate disagreements and life differences with grace, understanding that the friendship is more important than being right all the time.

The second level of acceptance has to do with people who are hard to love. Perhaps these people are more difficult to accept because their lives are very different from ours. Perhaps they frustrate or annoy us. Sometimes they hurt us, or they cause extra weariness in our lives. Friendship with them is not the mutually gratifying, helpful experience we've talked about in this book so far. But that doesn't mean there's not spiritual value in being friends with someone who is hard to love. In fact, God uses those people to develop our strength and character. He helps us learn patience and unselfish caring. As Luke 6:32-36 says,

If you only love the lovable, do you expect a pat on the back? Run-of-the-mill sinners do that. If you only help those who help you, do you expect a medal? Garden-variety sinners do that. If you only give for what you hope to get out of it, do you think that's charity? The stingiest of pawnbrokers does that.

I tell you, love your enemies. Help and give without expecting a return. You'll never—I promise—regret it. Live out this God-created identity the way our Father lives toward us, generously and graciously, even when we're at our worst. Our Father is kind; you be kind.

To connect with someone who is different from me, I get on their level. I do the things they're interested in, connect with them where they're at. It's incarnational living—choosing to "become flesh" where someone is at, not demanding they come to you and figure out your life instead. When people feel safe with you— when they feel seen and understood—they begin to trust you. Trust flowing back and forth in relationship is so crucial for this kind of spiritual friendship we've been talking about.

Of course, a person can get hurt living like that. When you accept another person at face value, you might get hurt or be used. And that's why it's important to be aware of the third level of acceptance: recognizing those who don't get the same kind of welcome into our lives because their role is not "safe."

We do need to be careful of some people. If someone has been abusive or hurt you deeply, you need to set good boundaries. Acceptance doesn't mean you set aside healthy limits or allow people in who are going to damage you or those you love. Sometimes it takes a while to realize that you need to set good boundaries with a person. Sometimes acceptance is accepting that someone will be better served by learning a hard lesson apart from you.

I have been fortunate—I have had only one bad relational experience in my whole life (though it was big and hurtful). I'm grateful that I've been able to live open to others, because in that posture of acceptance, I've seen the richest spiritual friendships emerge.

ACCEPTING OURSELVES

You don't need to be an extrovert to live open to others—our personalities don't have to determine how we choose to love and see other people. That's a decision we can each make. You may think, *Oh, but I'm shy and introverted* or *I don't even know how to go deep in a conversation*. But spiritual friendship isn't only for those who make friends easily or can strike up a conversation with the person in line at the grocery story. Spiritual friendship is simply about choosing to love people right as they are, choosing to invest in them.

If we hide away and think we can't do it because "that's just how I am," we're going to miss out on the true friendships we long for. That's why accepting ourselves—not wishing we were someone else—is so crucial for healthy friendships. No more hiding. No more feeling like you don't measure up. Who you are is just enough for the rich, deep friendships you long for.

My older sister was an introvert, a creative, the sort of person who loved to wander off by herself on long walks and just think. Years later, she told me that she had been envious of me when we were growing up because I had so many friends and she was a loner. That really surprised me. She was doing what she wanted to do, and I was too. I wished she could understand that being quiet and introspective didn't need to keep her from being cared for and known.

At the same time, over the course of my life, I have learned to accept that I am still in process. Choosing to accept whatever work God is doing in my life has helped me be open to new experiences and new ways of seeing myself and my relationships.

One year, Eugene suggested that the two of us go to Kirkridge Retreat Center in the Pocono Mountains of Pennsylvania for a weekend retreat on leisure time with the Quaker writer Douglas Steere. I wasn't quite sure what that meant, but any time away from the church and family and alone with my husband was a welcomed invitation. We made arrangements for my folks to stay with the children.

We drove up, arriving for the retreat late afternoon on a Friday. The retreat started with dinner, and the first gathering was right after. Douglas had us introduce and tell a little about ourselves—where we lived and worked and any other description that would be helpful to each other. Then he spoke for forty-five minutes or so about leisure time with God. He said the busyness, the distraction, and all the involvements of our lives often left out the most important part of our Christian life and faith.

And then he called us into silence for the whole weekend.

I told Eugene at bedtime (even though we were supposed to be in The Great Silence) that I didn't think I could not talk for the whole weekend. He comforted me by saying, "We can take a walk together on the Appalachian Trail tomorrow afternoon and talk some then." My dear husband, holding a carrot out before me.

The next morning, we all ate in silence through

breakfast. After Douglas spoke for a time, he sent us out to walk, journal, write, do whatever by ourselves. While at first I dreaded the prospect, this time was a whole new, wonderful beginning for me, for engaging with my inner life and learning how to be comfortable with me—Jan. As Eugene and I walked around the retreat grounds, others were doing the same. As we passed one another, I felt something between us that I had never felt before. We didn't greet each other as we might have done at the post office or grocery store. We were in silence—in The Great Silence—and it was good. Our spirits connected without saying anything or smiling at each other.

Eugene and I did take our walk on the trail in the afternoon, and we talked a little. But with no demands to make conversation, I found I didn't want to break the silence with my voice.

The mealtime was an eye opener. The colors of the food—the reds and yellows, the greens and oranges—just seemed so intense, leaping up off the plate at me. Eating in silence is not what we normally do, but I found I enjoyed the food and the quiet in a way that seemed almost natural to me. I eat slowly anyway, and having to make conversation with a table full of strangers is more awkward for me than eating in silence.

On Sunday morning, we came out of The Great Silence to share what transpired for each of us. I had been praying the Psalms during the weekend and had noted some phrases that had stayed with me: "Thou dost show me the path of life; in thy presence there is fullness of joy, in thy right hand are pleasures for evermore" (Psalm 16:11, rsv); "Answer me when I call, O God of my right! Thou hast given me room when I was in distress. Be gracious to me, and hear my prayer" (Psalm 4:1, rsv).

We returned home deeply refreshed and renewed, and I returned home a different person. I had been introduced to something that was too good to keep. I shared about the experience with my Bible study group and suggested that we go on a day of silent retreat together. We started our annual silent retreat that June and looked forward to it each year.

Our retreat day looked like this: We met at the

church after the children were all off on their school buses. We brought a light lunch, our Bibles, and a notebook. We carpooled north to a retreat and conference center and went to the pavilion down in the woods, away from other buildings, people, and noise. After we gathered together, I put on a tape about The Great Silence or read something that would prepare us for the quiet time. After a brief time, I sent them into The Silence until lunchtime. I rang a bell at that time as a sign to regather and eat together—again in The Silence. And if you don't think those first couple of years were hard for these women, you don't know women! But increasingly, they "got" it. They really entered into that time, walking in silence, sitting by the creek just being still and quiet, observing, listening to birdsong high in the treetops, sitting in the presence of our Maker. In that afternoon period, I instructed them to return to the pavilion after an hour so we could share what we experienced. It was always an intimate time of sharing. Then we packed ourselves into our cars to meet our kids as they came home from school. It may not have been a whole weekend like I had experienced, but we all experienced the benefits as the years went by.

I have become a much more introspective person, which I think probably happens naturally to extroverts as we age, but it has also been an intentional journey of accepting how God has grown me. I build on those past experiences and find I really do need to be quiet in the presence of God and to be alone with him. And I think this just might be God's way of preparing us for the end of our days on earth—for one day being with him with no interruptions.

The experience of becoming more introspective has impacted me greatly over the years. With all the technological "stuff" around us, I feel we should seize these kinds of opportunities whenever we can. We can do this kind of thing in home groups for just an evening. We can start small! By learning to connect with God in the silence, learning to become more introspective—no matter our personality—we become more able in understanding and accepting of ourselves, which leads us to become more accepting of others.

When we're relating with friends, we accept them for who they are and what they talk about. But in order to approach these relationships with open hearts, we need to learn to accept ourselves. Accepting how God has created us will allow us to invest in our relationship without jealousy or judgment. None of us can change overnight. We are all in the process of becoming.

1. Have you had a friendship with someone who was very different from you? What did you learn from that experience?

2. Think of a friend whom you'd place in the first level of acceptance (someone more similar to you, with whom it's easy to connect). What have you learned about acceptance from that person?

3. Think of a friend whom you'd place in the second level of acceptance (someone with whom you've had to work a bit harder to develop a friendship). What have you learned about acceptance from that person?

4. Have you ever had to use discernment to set boundaries with an unsafe person in your life? What did you learn from that situation?

5. What has been hardest for you to accept about yourself? What could you do to better understand the beauty of how God has created you?

CHAPTER 3

SERVICE

Caring in Action

Don't burn out; keep yourselves fueled and aflame.
Be alert servants of the Master, cheerfully expectant.
Don't quit in hard times; pray all the harder.

ROMANS 12:11-12

Iᶠ I ᴜɴᴅᴇʀsᴛᴀɴᴅ Jesus rightly, when, on the night of his betrayal, he washed the disciples' feet and told them to love one another and serve one another, I think he was showing us, his followers, that this is what we are to do also. In one way or another, we are

45

to serve and love one another. There are no elevated positions in this Kingdom work.

Service is so crucial in spiritual friendship. As we talked about before, caring is action. And we call that action *service*! You can't separate caring from service in spiritual friendship—without service, caring is superficial, and without caring, service has no heart. In serving someone, we're demonstrating that we mean what we say. When we love someone, we want to do what's best for them. Service is intentional, focused on the needs of someone else. It cultivates a willingness in our hearts to see the people around us and always think of what we can do for them. And accepting the servant hearts of others cultivates humility in us. We learn to see the value and love of others when we aren't too proud to let them serve us as well.

Service can be intimidating for some of us, because we may look at what another person is doing and feel like what we have to offer isn't nearly as good. We need to remember: Some of us are called in certain ways to serve, but we are all called to be servants, whatever our gifts are. No one's gift is more significant than anyone else's!

Uniquely Called

Eugene had to convince me over a period of years that my calling to be a pastor's wife was just as important, if not more so, as his of being a pastor. It was the 1960s, and good ol' Betty Friedan was on every talk show, telling us women that we must exert and express ourselves and not let men put us down. But even when women began leaving the home in droves to go into the workforce, God used that tension to allow me to say to myself, "But this is what I really want to do. This is what God has called me to do— serve my husband and my church, my children and my community." And I thank God to this day that I have stayed with what I perceived as my calling. I was called to a different kind of service than some of the women around me.

Though I have desired to serve, it has probably only been in the last twenty years or so that I have come to understand what my gifts are and what those gifts look like in serving others. But I take heart in meeting people like Father Kilian McDonnell, a Benedictine monk at St. John's Abbey in Collegeville, Minnesota, and reading his books of poems, which he started writing at the age of seventy-five. And I am reminded of Grandma Moses, who started painting her humble but lovely country scenes at the age of seventy-eight. Wendell Berry, in his poetry book *Leavings*, reminds me that I am not old but new, that each new phase of my life is just that—new.[4] I've never been "here" before. Each phase of my bodily changes is "new," not old. So I take heart and receive encouragement from fellow pilgrims such as these, friends who are as old as or older than me and continue to venture forth in new beginnings.

My life—indeed, what I think of as my identity— is serving others. So except for speaking at an occasional retreat I have led over the years or writing many letters and notes of encouragement to friends and acquaintances in need of gifts of love and relationship, my life, at least in the past sixty years of marriage, has been about serving others: serving family, serving friends, serving our community, and serving whatever congregation God has called us to.

In 1962, we moved with our two-year-old daughter to a new congregation Eugene was called to start for the Presbyterian Church (U.S.A.) in a rural area of Harford County, twenty miles northeast of Baltimore, Maryland. We had been blessed and sent off by the White Plains Presbyterian Church in New York, where we had been serving as associate pastor and wife for the previous three years. It was there that Eugene terminated his doctoral dissertation work while under the leadership of Dr. and Mrs. William J. Wiseman, as he realized for the first time in his life that this pastoral calling was authentic, in-the-trenches work. For Eugene, there was so much more richness of life and life's issues in the church than in the classroom. He knew that this was his calling in life—to be a pastor. He knew that he had been a pastor all his life but had no models to recognize himself in until working with Bill Wiseman. Now, together as a young pastor and pastor's wife, we began learning together just what this calling was and how to live it. (And how not to do it!)

Because Maryland was originally settled as a Catholic colony, we now had a distinct separation of church and state and therefore could not use a public school to rent for our services on Sunday mornings. Our presbytery's New Church Development leaders recommended that we settle in the neighborhood where they had purchased over six acres of land four years earlier for a new church site—and that we purchase a house with a large basement to hold our services. The Board of National Missions paid the down payment (we were missionaries!) and our full salary for one year. They would continue making house payments and paying our salary, dropping it by a third each year for the new church to pick up and pay. So, by the end of three years, the church would be self-supporting. I thought that that was a good way to do it, and thankfully, our little flock was able to cover the cost of our housing and salary. The rub for me, though, was that the salary offer was $2,000 less than we had been making in White Plains, and our little family of three was soon going to add a new family member. We had been making $7,500 a year as associate pastor, and now we were making less while organizing and hosting a new church in our home. It was a lot more work and personal involvement!

During those years, I learned that I loved serving people through our home. I didn't mind having the church meet in our basement—at all! I was glad to be able to serve people and welcome people. Yes, it was a bit of work (especially since we couldn't afford a dryer, and I had to hang the diapers up in the basement and then take them down before the deacons came over), but I liked it. (I think I could have afforded a dryer if it hadn't been for John Wilson, who went to our church. He worked at the furniture store, and when I went to look at a dryer, he stood in front of this beautiful red desk as we talked. I kept looking at that desk instead of him, so I got that desk instead of a dryer. I always blamed John Wilson for our not having a dryer for several years.)

When we went to teach at Regent College in Vancouver, Canada, I loved serving people in our home because it was something that I could do for the students. It meant that it wasn't just Eugene who was called to Regent; I had a place there where I could invest in the students. All the faculty wives were attentive to the school and students. This was a surprise to me, that anybody would want to seek me out and spend time one-on-one with me, and a lot of students and spouses of students particularly did. Toward the end of one group's time at Regent, they asked if we could keep in touch by writing round-robin letters, so we did that for at least two years. I gave them encouragement and helped them adjust to their new roles. They would talk about what they were going through, and I saw my particular service as supporting them in their new life stage. It was very, very sweet and very helpful. And then other people in the community seemed to take to me as well.

I've also found serving to be a consistent thread in my role as a wife and mother. I've always put my hands to the plow and done what was needed to take care of my family. As so many women before me (such as my mother and mother-in-law, to name two) have done, I learned how to cook seasonally and use powdered milk rather than whole milk in my cooking. I cut and used coupons for things we would buy anyway and bought cheaper cuts of meat that meant having to cook them longer (but that's when my slow cooker came to the rescue). I cooked closer to the source, using none of those Hamburger Helper or other expensive boxes of helpful and time-saving aids. I've since learned that those inner aisles of the grocery store are not good for us, with all the additives that lengthen shelf life, and that the outside wall edges are where we can find the whole foods that are healthier for us. At that time, I was spending fifty cents a day per family member for food, if you can believe it. Of course, food prices are much higher today, so that same food would cost a lot more now. But I was learning about food and how to prepare it, reading every recipe I could get my hands on and experimenting with herbs and spices. I learned economical wisdom that I have never forgotten or given up. When food prices soared in the '60s and '70s, my challenge became even keener. I am glad I learned early, because two years after our son Eric was born, baby brother Leif joined us in the house church.

If you are a wife and mother, then you know this kind of service all too well. It may look different for you, but each of us learns to sacrifice to serve our family. We make meals at the end of the day, we clean, we do laundry, and sometimes it feels like it never ends. But this is an act of service, and there is spiritual value to this rhythm of loving our families well.

Some of us may feel that our service is limited by our role—that we need to serve in ways that people expect of us. I certainly wrestled with this as a pastor's wife. In my era, people had strong opinions about what a pastor's wife should or should not be doing— the pastor's wife played the piano and was the one who poured tea at the women's meetings. (I told Eugene when we were still in the dating days that I didn't play the piano. It didn't seem to be an issue with him, thankfully.) I would have hoped that by now, pastors' wives would be accepted for who they are, but as I spend time with the younger ones today, I hear some

of the same things still going on. My young friend
Debbie told me that one of their parishioners said
to her, "In our last church, the pastor's wife did such
and such," suggesting that Debbie should be doing
that too. Debbie asked me, "How should I respond
to that kind of thing?" I told Debbie to just thank
her and say something like "She must have been a
wonderful woman." And leave it at that. I encouraged
her to live her life as a pastor's wife, serving out of
her faith journey and her own gifts, not out of others'
expectations. And she does. Debbie has her own gifts.
She's her own person. She serves not because anyone
told her to, but because that's where she's called. As
a young person, you have to discover your gifts. You
don't know what all your gifts are until you grow up.
When expectations are imposed on you, you can't discover those gifts.

When it comes to how and where I've been called
to serve, I frankly couldn't and can't be something I'm
not deep within myself. I am Jan. What you see is what
you get. As we open up our hearts to the Lord, I believe
he "grows" us in our gifts and how we should serve. He

knows our hearts and our desires and is true to us. You have been created with unique gifts and a unique call to serve right where you are. What things has God placed on your heart? How have you been created? Lean in to those things and see what God wants to do as you serve others.

Of course, standing firm in who we are and serving from how we've been created doesn't mean we should step on toes. I try to be the loving servant God has called me to be, even if I feel I am being criticized or not accepted in that way. There are some people we will never be able to please. And, really, we are here to please our heavenly Father. As long as we follow his lead in how we use our gifts to serve others, we are serving just as we ought.

The Ripple Effect of Service

The amazing thing about service is that it rarely returns void, even if we don't see the end results ourselves. Service has a way of inspiring others to see the areas of need around them and step out of their comfort zones to help someone else. Eugene and I saw this happen in a beautiful way during one particular season of serving.

Our friend David and his wife, Janet, were in our church from the very beginning. She was our organist. Theirs was a blended marriage; they each had three children. Tragically, Janet got cancer and passed away, leaving David with all those children to care for. David had a good job and was working in Baltimore, but before Janet died, the company got moved to the West Coast. His hands were tied. He couldn't move his dying wife and kids at that time, so he ended up getting a job that financially didn't allow him and the children to stay in their house. At first, the grandmother took the kids up to Pennsylvania, where she lived, but they were very unhappy there. They were used to living in their hometown, and they wanted to be with their father.

So my dear, blessed husband said to David, "Well, we'll take them in." Two of the children had already left home, so we welcomed the younger four—three boys and one girl—into our home, in addition to our three children. Our daughter, Karen, was ten, and our boys were two and three years younger. It was a houseful! We only had three bedrooms. Thankfully, by that time, the church had been built, so we no longer had anyone in the basement. The whole basement was empty except for Eugene's workshop and study. We put the boys down in the basement, and the girl shared a bedroom with Karen.

Those children were with us for about three months. And it went okay. The septic tank overflowed, so we had to figure out what to do there. We carted the kids back and forth to the church to use the bathroom! That's the thing about service: It's not easy. A lot of times, you're going to serve when you don't feel up for it. I had to fix seven school lunches when we really couldn't afford to buy lunch for everybody. There I was in the morning, preparing all these lunches and getting breakfast for the kids and sending them to the school bus—it was overwhelming! So Eugene organized the kids so they helped with packing their lunches. But you get tired in the midst of a heavy service season, when you wonder, *How long?*

But here's what bolstered us in the midst of that season: As we were living lives of sacrificial service, the church began to do the same. Prior to this, Eugene had tried to get people in the church to be aware of others who were going through a hard time. He'd make phone calls, asking for things like meals for new parents, trying to create a community of service. No one seemed to want that sort of community.

But then we took in the children. The church couldn't believe it. People seemed overtaken by the idea of service—and they started pitching in. People started bringing food to the front door. The deacons said, "We can't let the Petersons just feed these kids out of their living," so they started giving us extra money for food. Somebody gave us bunk beds and a cot for the boys. And, sweetly, a family in the church invited David to come and live with them until he could get a place for both him and the kids.

When we had been longing for community, community suddenly appeared. That's because service creates a community of giving. We never had to make another phone call.

A Life of Serving

When I think about being a servant, serving in Jesus' name, I am reminded of a favorite verse from Luke 1:37-38. The angel Gabriel was visiting Mary, telling her she would be the mother of Jesus, "Son of the Highest." And he also told her about her cousin Elizabeth, who was old and barren but was now pregnant with a son. The angel said, "Nothing, you see, is impossible with God." And Mary said, "Yes, I see it all now: I'm the Lord's maid, ready to serve. Let it be with me just as you say." And so this should be our attitude as well! Whether we are serving the Lord or serving others in our families and friendships, our service should be unfettered, open, and willing. It's such a strong response. We should be ready to spring into action, loving our friends in concrete and active ways. Just like Mary, we should have the courage to serve where God calls us, which may not be in the ways the people around us expect. And we should be humble and willing to accept the help and service of others, just as Mary accepted the love and service of

Elizabeth, who encouraged and lifted up Mary in the midst of a time when no one else understood her.

May we all have the desire to serve God in Mary's spirit! *Fiat mihi*—may it be unto me. Amen.

REFLECTIONS ON

Service

⟨————————⟩

1. Do you find service a natural rhythm of your life or something a bit more difficult? Why do you think that is?

2. How have you been uniquely equipped for service? That is, where do you find it easy to step in and love others through serving? How have you felt limited by your role?

3. What have you learned about consistent serving through your closest relationships?

4. Consider a time when someone else's actions spurred you on to "love and good deeds" (Hebrews 10:24, NIV). What did you learn about service during that situation?

5. What reaction do you have to Mary's words in Luke 1:38? How might you better apply them right now in your life?

CHAPTER 4

HOSPITALITY
Reaching Out and Bringing In

Help needy Christians;
be inventive in hospitality. . . .
Make friends with nobodies;
don't be the great somebody.

ROMANS 12:13, 16

$\mathcal{W}$HY SHOULD I practice hospitality in spiritual friendship? To me, hospitality is a natural thing you do in friendship. You open your home to your friend whenever she needs to come to you—and she would do the same for you. Hospitality is a way to support someone in the midst of hard times, acting as a haven for them, helping and encouraging in tangible ways. And the vulnerability and service that come through opening your home and welcoming someone in is a foundational part of spiritual friendship. You're welcoming someone into a precious place as an act of love.

I remember realizing several years ago, as I knelt at the Communion rail to receive the bread and wine—the body and blood of our Lord—that this is God's hospitable gift to and for me. It was a profound moment for me: God has blessed me with the gift of hospitality, and yet there I was in my sixties, experiencing consciously for the first time his hospitality for me in this act of kneeling and receiving. I feel so humbled when I receive this gift he has given to me.

Hospitality is a misunderstood art, I think, because it is so often removed from relationship. When I see the word *hospitality* in the food section of the newspaper, I think that our culture has missed the true meaning. Resorts and hotels offer "hospitality," but they only borrow the word. True hospitality is not a business. Hospitality as expressed by our Lord is healing, breaking bread, blessing, giving, welcoming the little children. So I get a little miffed when I see the word used to serve corporate purposes and pocketbooks.

A good definition of hospitality is *the welcoming reception and treatment of guests and strangers in a warm, friendly, generous way.* In his book *Reaching Out*, Henri Nouwen says the best hospitality is when you can't tell the difference between the host and the guest.[5] Like so many other aspects of spiritual friendship, hospitality is giving and receiving in a continuous flow. When we offer hospitality, our guest, whether a friend or a stranger, gives us something in return.

One of the best experiences I have ever had was in a soup kitchen on Queen Anne Hill in Seattle years ago. The church members prepare a very tasty meal in the church kitchen every Wednesday night. When they first started this program for the homeless, something like twenty people came. Now, over two hundred homeless people take part. It's a beautiful time of service and hospitality, with delicious food and linen tablecloths on the serving tables. But the best part is that the people from the church have supper at the tables with these folks, and conversation and friendships emerge. The humanity of those the world often overlooks is highlighted and celebrated.

When Eugene and I were invited to attend and help with the serving, one of the guests was playing the piano. At one point while the man was playing, I went over and talked with him. He was excited because one of the church members had promised to bring his violin the next week so they could play together during the supper. I was grateful for our conversation and grateful to see this man's gifts at work. He was offering lovely music to hosts and guests alike. When he left at the end of the evening, I said, "Good-bye, Chris." And he, surprised that I remembered his name, surprised me by saying, "Good-bye, Jan." He and the other guests were giving back to the church as they received from the church—through their gifts and through their relationships. I left that evening feeling more like the person that I want to become.

"The paradox of hospitality," Nouwen writes in

Reaching Out, "is that it wants to create emptiness, not a fearful emptiness, but a friendly emptiness where strangers can enter and discover themselves as created free; free to sing their own songs, speak their own languages, dance their own dances; free also to leave and follow their own vocations. Hospitality is not a subtle invitation to adopt the life style of the host, but the gift of a chance for the guest to find his own."[6] When hospitality is done well like this, you experience something profound. Something like the Jewish word *shalom*—a sense of wholeness, where more is present than what you see.

This is why hospitality is so important in spiritual friendship. We create wholeness in relationship when we welcome others. In the deepest, richest friendships, each of us is released to be ourselves, to offer others what gifts we have, to serve and love and care. Friendship also gives us the opportunity to reach out and honor how God has made others, creating an environment in which they can flourish. Our friends are always welcome, always taken care of, always shown generosity in relationship and hospitality. And, of course, in spiritual friendships, this should go both ways. We are completely ourselves, working together to offer hospitality to each other.

HOSPITALITY IN SCRIPTURE

Jesus showed us the deeper reason why hospitality is so vital to the life of faith: "Whenever you did one of these things to someone overlooked or ignored, that was me—you did it to me" (Matthew 25:40). Welcoming others, offering them a place of safety and home, is the way of Jesus. And more than that, it's so important to Jesus, he says that showing hospitality to others is the same as showing it to him. What a high calling!

Aspects of the Rule of St. Benedict emerge from this call to treat all people as you would treat Christ. Benedict was a monk who lived in the sixth century, and hospitality played an important role in the monastic tradition he established. Perhaps he based his approach to hospitality on the story of Abraham welcoming the three strangers.[7]

When you live in the desert, you are expected to extend hospitality to guests who show up at your oasis and the flap of your tent. That's why Abraham didn't hesitate when three strangers arrived. He cooked a fine meal and invited them to eat! Abraham didn't know these strangers were special until they made an amazing announcement: They would return this time next year, when Sarah would have a baby. Now, this was astounding news—Abraham had been hearing this promise from God for a very long time. God had told Abraham that he would bless him and Sarah with a son and that their descendants would be as many as the grains of sand on the seashore and the stars in the sky. This poor couple had waited and waited for that promise to come to fruition, but now they were both old—Sarah was well past menopause—and they were supposed to believe that?

If you know the story well, you probably remember that Sarah was at the tent flap, listening in on the conversation with the visitors . . . and she laughed. (I guess I would have too.) But Abraham took the strangers' words seriously. He knew he had been visited by three angels. We think of those three as the Father, the Son, and the Holy Spirit. Many years later, the writer of Hebrews looked back at this story to emphasize the importance of hospitality, saying, "Be ready with a meal or a bed when it's needed. Why, some have extended hospitality to angels without ever knowing it" (Hebrews 13:2).

Hospitality is still a part of life in the desert, as Eugene and I experienced when we were in the Negev with a tour group a number of years ago. As we drove up to the home of a Bedouin family, the women opened their homes to us. First, we went into the main living area and sat there in chairs, and the woman of the house spoke and allowed us to ask questions about their way of life. Then, she took us to the next tent over, which had a fire in the middle of the room, and we sat around the edge while the women cooked for us. They passed the food around the edge of the fire so we could all eat. The next tent we went to was the men's tent, and they welcomed us with coffee. Abundant and intentional hospitality—and I think that these people would regularly do this for visitors.

In the midst of being welcomed by strangers, we were reminded of what Jesus told the rich young lawyer. The man asked Jesus how to enter the Kingdom of God, and Jesus asked in return, "What is written in the Law?"

The young man told him, "'Love the Lord your God with all your heart and with all your soul and with all your strength and with all your mind'; and, 'Love your neighbor as yourself.'"

Jesus then said, "You have answered correctly. . . . Do this and you will live."

But the rich young man asked Jesus, "And who is my neighbor?"[8]

Jesus then told him the story of the Good Samaritan. You likely know the story well: A man was beaten and robbed. The role-playing ones (the religious ones—the Levite and the priest) passed by on the other side of the road and pretended not to see him. I've walked on that road, the Jericho Road from Jerusalem. It's very narrow. The priest and the Levite would have almost had to step over the man. Along came a Samaritan, the impure and despised one. He knelt down, bandaged the hurt man, and took him to the inn. When someone is bleeding and hurting, we must, like the Good Samaritan, seize the opportunity to serve, to help bind up the wounds. We should not just extend hospitality to those whom we like or who like us. Nor should we extend hospitality only when it's convenient or on our own terms. Hospitality can't wait until we feel like doing it. If it did depend on our feelings and readiness, we might just never practice it—and we would miss out on tremendous growth and blessings.

THE GIFT OF HOSPITALITY

When I offer hospitality, something amazing happens—so much more than I have anything to do with. An exchange takes place. Our guests bring who they are with them and enlarge our lives in their offerings. When we offer guests space, a lot of creative growth occurs.

Eugene and I don't "entertain," as such. We might go hiking, take a walk with our guests, or take a swim with them, but we don't "show them a great time," so to speak.

What I do before they arrive is the usual—prepare beds and get a little dust off of things, plan and shop for meals, maybe place a few wild flowers in their room, some extra little touches to show we care about them. But we basically leave them alone while they're here. We always have good, rich conversations around the table at mealtime. Giving people space and a listening ear and heart are often rare in today's world. And people are hungry for it, whether they're aware of it or not.

The apostle Paul reminds us in Romans 12:13, "Be inventive in hospitality." The sky's the limit. There are various ways we can extend hospitality in our world today. Smiling at people you pass in the store or on the street. A simple act, but sometimes it makes a big difference to someone who is not feeling very well that day. Holding the door open at the post office for someone coming in, greeting people you may or may not know. These simple acts of kindness done in the spirit of Jesus can and do make a difference.

When I was in high school, Gertrude gave me a little book entitled *Try Giving Yourself Away.*[9] I don't have my copy after all these years, but what I remember is that it was full of stories of people who were encouragers to others. Like writing to an author and thanking him or her for their writing, or telling someone else what they see in the other person that stands out, or writing notes and letters to friends who are going through a hard time in their lives.

The idea of trying to give myself away has stuck through the years as a particularly effective form of hospitality. I remember my friend Lu doing that with the visitors to our church, asking them questions about themselves, showing an interest in them. After observing her, I made a concerted effort to start doing that myself. I guess you might say I got out of myself, my self-centeredness, or I stepped aside enough to provide space for the other person.

Giving yourself away doesn't have to be a big thing—just an intentional one, an action that shows love and awareness of the other person. I'm reminded of the year our son and his family treated Eugene and me to an afternoon performance of *The Sound of Music* for Christmas. During the intermission, our ten-year-old granddaughter Mary asked her grandfather what he wanted for Christmas. He said, "Silence!" She looked at him kind of funny, then turned to her father and said, "Grampa wants silence for Christmas." They chuckled, and nothing more was said. Two weeks later, when our son brought down their dog for us to tend to while they went to Ohio for Christmas, Leif handed Eugene a large box and said, "This is from Mary." Eugene opened it up and inside found a piece of paper folded in fourths. He unfolded the paper, and it had been colored on both sides of the paper with a yellow crayon. On it, Mary had written, "Merry Christmas, Granddad, and a Happy New Year. Silence is golden or yellow." Then, at the bottom of the paper—"HA-HA-HA." In a small, perhaps silly way, Mary was learning to give herself away—remembering what her grandfather wanted and finding a creative way to give it to him.

So you see, I'm simply suggesting using our

imaginations and being creative in our giving. You'll be surprised at how much a person will be touched by something unexpected coming their way and what a lift it will give them. But you will get a lift as well. It's really fun. Sometimes if you try to give an old grouch a gift of imagination, it may backfire on you, but sometimes, that touches them in the deepest places of their hearts. They're surprised that someone is thinking about them and caring for them.

But we cannot show true hospitality if it's not in every aspect of our life. Have you thought about what it means to be hospitable to your family? That seems strange to ask, doesn't it? But we perhaps need to think about that, for it is here, in our families, that hospitality makes the most difference to our world. In our families, we are not only learning to show hospitality on a daily basis but also passing it on in a consistent and faithful way. Hospitality in our families can be as simple as preparing an evening meal and having the whole family sit around the table, sharing in the food and in each others' company.

Albert Borgmann, who works in the philosophy

department at the University of Montana, talks about focal practices, which he defines as something of ultimate importance that counters the modern distractions of technology.[10] The Latin word *foci*, from which the word *focal* comes, means "hearth." The hearth is a focal practice. Before we had furnaces in our homes where all you have to do is turn on a switch, you had to gather wood, cut it, split it, bring it in to the fireplace or the woodstove, cook over it, keep it stoked during the day, and when it got dark at night, you put more wood on the fire and went to bed. The whole family was involved in the focal practice of the hearth. Another focal practice that many have again picked up in their families is the vegetable garden. I used to have our kids help after the harvest by making pickles with me, getting the tomatoes picked and ready for Eugene and me to make tomato juice and canned tomatoes for the winter. I never knew I was doing something called "focal practice" at the time, but we sure had a lot of fun doing it together as a family.

Many of the focal practices are a thing of the

past, and if we let the evening meal go, we are letting one more focal practice disappear. The evening meal is where we can be hospitable to each other—asking about each other's day, talking about people we saw and conversations we had, sharing about things we learned at school. When my fifteen-year-old grandson heard me bemoaning the fact that so few families have an evening meal together and how that must be having a ripple effect on our brokenness, he said, "That's the only time when we see each other all together each day." He felt that it was really important. Around the same time, I heard that the one thing all the most recent National Merit Scholars had in common was the family evening meal. Does that sound as though something significant might go on in those homes around those evening dinnertimes? When we show hospitality to our family, we are developing the practice to give beyond ourselves—and we are modeling hospitality to those who are watching us most closely and see us every day.

I've discovered that when you make a decision to

show hospitality and start acting on that decision, the first step is a huge one. It leads to other acts of kindness and more and more creative acts. As we practice, something gets freed up inside us, and hospitality becomes more and more natural in our day-to-day living.

The apostle Paul's treatise on freedom from the epistle to the Galatians reads like this in *The Message*:

> It is absolutely clear that God has called you
> to a free life. Just make sure that you don't use
> this freedom as an excuse to do whatever you
> want to do and destroy your freedom. Rather,
> use your freedom to serve one another in love;
> that's how freedom grows. For everything
> we know about God's Word is summed up
> in a single sentence: Love others as you love
> yourself. That's an act of true freedom.
>
> GALATIANS 5:13-14

True hospitality should emerge out of that beautiful freedom.

THE HOSPITABLE LIFE

I grew up in a hospitable family. Mother often welcomed guests into our home. I especially remember her asking my friends over for my birthdays and letting me have them spend the night, too. I think of my father as being one of the last real gentlemen. Daddy always treated everyone with respect and kindness, accepting people into our lives. Watching the gift of hospitality in action as a child has influenced me my whole life.

Now we live in a world of rush, rush, where everybody seems so busy. And we live in a highly technical world, one that depersonalizes us. We text or talk on our cell phones to a person not present, and the people present to us are cut off entirely. I remember years ago a book with the title *The Lonely Crowd* that addressed this same kind of thing.[11] But today's isolation is so much more pervasive. Hospitality is hard in times like these because it requires us to slow down and choose to open our homes and our hearts to others.

But spiritual friendship can only thrive within a

life of hospitality. Hospitality isn't about us; it's about the person who comes into our home as a guest. When we choose to welcome people into our lives, to make them feel themselves and at home, we create space for depth and beauty to emerge in us and them. Friendship grows best in intentionality, and hospitality is the warmest kind of intentionality there is.

REFLECTIONS ON

Hospitality

⟨————————————⟩

1. In what ways do you practice hospitality in your life?

2. Have you ever considered Communion an act of God's
   hospitality toward us? What does reframing the body
   and blood in this way teach you about God?

3. Is hospitality a consistent part of your relationships?
   If not, what things are barriers to your development in
   hospitality?

4. In what ways have you been enriched by the exchange that happens in hospitality?

5. What is one way you can be inventive in hospitality this week?

CHAPTER 5

ENCOURAGEMENT

Building Others Up

Bless your enemies; no cursing under your breath.
Laugh with your happy friends when they're
happy; share tears when they're down. Get along
with each other; don't be stuck-up. Make friends
with nobodies; don't be the great somebody.

ROMANS 12:14-16

CHURCH LIFE HAS not always been an easy thing
for Eugene and me. Once, when we returned from
vacation, one of our elders picked us up at the airport
and said, "You have weeds growing in your garden."

He was gently but directly alerting us to discouraging unrest in the congregation. Two people in the church were saying, "We didn't hire Eugene to write books." Now, he wasn't writing on church time. My husband is an honorable man who uses his gifts wisely and well. So those words were very hurtful to me. I was also discouraged because I had relationships with these people. I took care of their kids. They were friends of our family. But what stands out to me about that time was that the elder chose to be such a source of encouragement to us. He spoke truth and affirmed Eugene. He and his wife had us over for meals. They were very dear to us.

Encouragement is such a vital part of our lives, isn't it? The world tears you down. I suspect you know this well. Life is hard. People can be unkind. I've often found that *Christians* can be unkind, and that's even more hurtful, because they are the people you should be able to rely on. That's why spiritual friends are so valuable—in the midst of all the hurt, in the midst of discouragement, they can speak words of hope and value right where you are. A healthy spiritual friendship reminds you of who you are, reminds you of the good. A good spiritual friend builds us up, identifying the good things God has done and is doing in our life.

An encouraging word on a hard day is like food to a starving person. Encouragement gives us the strength to move forward, no matter what we're facing. It helps us see ourselves as God sees us. I remember so clearly when Mother told me on one of her visits, "You have really become a beautiful woman." I felt just washed in blessing. In my family, we loved each other well, but words like that were special. It wasn't everyday stuff. When my mom said that to me, it was such a gift. Her words affirmed the work God was doing in me as a woman and continue to provide me with encouragement to this day.

Learning how to encourage others is so vital to our friendships. We help our friends become healthy and whole by speaking words of life to them. So how do we encourage each other well? We give support, confidence, or hope in active and vocal ways. Support can look like cheering a friend on in a new endeavor or speaking truth when they're beaten down by lies. Confidence can be calling out the gifts and good things they have to offer in order to show them they do have what it takes to face what's in front of them. Hope is a gift in dark places, an opportunity to point our friends toward life in the light.

The Encouraged Life

I was blessed to grow up in a culture of encouragement, which I think helped more naturally develop my sensitivity to this aspect of spiritual friendship. The people around me loved me well and encouraged me through investing in my life, which created in me an openheartedness and innocence that has been with me ever since. Because I was the third child in our family, the personal touch and care meant a great deal to me.

Some of my early encouragers included Martha and Ernest Thomson, the parents of my best childhood girlfriend in Birmingham, Alabama, who welcomed me in their home many times over the years.

And then there was Mrs. Clisby, our next-door neighbor, who stood me up on a chair in front of the kitchen sink and taught me how to wash dishes. And, of course, in my teen years, Gertrude, who welcomed me and treated me with so much kindness.

Our church was also a place of encouragement. The families in that place were generous with their friendship and love from the time I was young. Gladys Rucker, who was our Sunday school superintendent when I was in primary school, loved children and brought the best out of us as she gathered our primary department to sing and shared the love of Jesus with us. A deacon at the church, Mr. Pierce, always greeted the young people as we arrived for Sunday school and church each week. His care for and interest in each one of us made us feel at home.

It's an encouragement to know you're wanted and valued, for people in the congregation to reach out and treat you like a person, somebody that they notice and are glad to see. We can all do this—it doesn't have to be a very big thing. It's just choosing to be intentional in the small ways we reach out to others.

Our church was small and very personable. We had many ways of experiencing the love of Jesus at that little white clapboard Presbyterian church. My parents were both very involved in the life of the church, showing me how to offer encouragement in return by investing in relationships. Mother played the piano in one of the departments and helped with Vacation Bible School each summer. Daddy was an elder and served as Sunday school superintendent. He also taught a boys' high-school class. And my parents' relational investments came back to bless us, because healthy spiritual friendship and love is always reciprocal. For example, between Sunday school and church, the high-school boys Daddy taught would carry us little kids around on their backs. Sometimes, several of us would slip off to Doc Timerson's drugstore just down the street and get one of those Y-shaped ice-cream cones for a nickel (which was supposed to be my offering for church!).

I was nourished by so many people in my growing-up years. I think of little children being abused or yelled at, jerked around by their angry parents, and it makes me sad. I was encouraged to be myself. Yes, I was taught to be polite, to say, "yes, ma'am" and "no, ma'am" and to obey my parents, but I respected them so much, I didn't want to hurt them. We had a lot of good family time together, working puzzles and playing Parcheesi and Monopoly and other board games. We never had much money—this being right after the Great Depression—but we spent a lot of time with each other. Looking back, the one thing we didn't have was age-appropriate books to read. When we moved to Montgomery when I was ten years old, we had a Carnegie library not far away, and I would take a city bus down to it. But my parents did as well as they could. When I had my own children, I made sure we had plenty of good books.

But books or no books, my childhood was good. There were a lot of children in our neighborhood, and we played hard. I grew up with an abundance of relationship, an abundance of happy life with other people, and I think that set the tone for the rest of my life. In the summer months, we would play hide-and-seek, kick the can, and Mother May I? after supper until it got dark or we were called in by our parents. Irving Road was paved with concrete, so that was a smooth surface to learn to roller skate on, except when you would hit one of the street seams the wrong way. I wore out many a pair of underpants falling down until I mastered those seams. Because the Second World War started when I was five years old, I never had my own bicycle until I was ten years old, when they started manufacturing bikes again. But I learned on my older friends' bikes, so I knew how to ride when my dad was able to get me one at the end of the war.

The kids in our neighborhood had great imaginations. We wrote plays about Dracula and had our star drag a chain across our garage's concrete floor to make it as scary as we could for the smaller kids. We charged a nickel entrance fee but included refreshments. (A nickel was big income for us!)

We would take hikes over the hill to Cave Rock, exploring the hills and woods. We never knew what experience we might have. That was what made it so exciting and fun for us little people. One time, a herd of wild pigs came charging down the hill toward us on the path! Another time we saw a smoldering fire in a fire ring that we should have doused, because the next morning, when we awoke, the fire had come onto the hill where we had kite contests each spring, which was just above our home! But it was very exciting to watch the firemen with their fire trucks and water hoses fighting the fire. There was always some exciting thing going on, and if there wasn't, we made some up.

Like so many other parts of my childhood, our neighborhood was full of caring people. We kids always had such fun trick-or-treating on Halloween. All our neighbors were so kind and fun, admiring our costumes and handing out treats.

After our big Sunday dinner after church (all I wanted to do was go out and play with my friends), Daddy would pile us all into the car and take us for our weekly Sunday afternoon drive. For my brother and sister and me, our favorite thing was to drive south to where our good friends the Mabrys lived on a farm. We played and learned all about farm life and were even taught how to milk a cow. We always stayed for a light supper with our friends and, of course, the best thing of all: helping churn homemade ice cream. The Mabrys were a loving part of my childhood that helped build the foundation of encouragement and friendship.

My innocence got nourished. My spirit grew. There was so much support, love, and encouragement all around me in my growing-up years that I look back and marvel and can only thank God for giving me such an uncomplicated and simple life.

Perhaps the most defining point of hope and encouragement in my life was when I was given the opportunity to ask Jesus to live in my heart. Two seminary students home for the weekend met with our youth fellowship; they dimmed the lights, lit a candle on the table in front, and invited us into the quiet presence of God. I had been through confirmation class and had just become a member of the church but had never been given the opportunity to receive Jesus before. I remember praying that night, "I want to love and serve you all the days of my life. Please help me to love and serve you all my life long. Please help me to live for you." I have always been grateful for that evening, for the ability to look back and find ongoing encouragement from God's continued work in me.

I write all of this to show how blessed I was to receive an abundance of love and encouragement that I could then pass on to others. For most of my life, I've been able to offer friendship out of a full tank, if you will. Not everyone has a story like mine. There's an incredible strength in learning how to speak life and hope to someone else when you yourself feel like you're worn thin. That's why spiritual friendship is so important. We are better givers when we are able to receive. Our friends can be those who fill us up, who build encouragement into our lives, so that we can then do the same in theirs and others'.

FINDING ENCOURAGEMENT IN GOD'S FAITHFULNESS

In my life, one of the most consistent sources of encouragement has been God's faithfulness. Our God works in deeply encouraging ways, walking alongside us and working even when we can't see it. Faithfulness is retrospective: We often don't see God working in the moment, but we can reflect over our lives and see him moving in every step and every season. After eight decades of life, I can vouch for that. If you are discouraged right now, take a look back. See what God has done before, and know that he is taking care of you still.

It brings a smile to my face to reflect on a particularly sweet season of God's faithfulness, when I was discouraged about one story ending—and then so encouraged as God led me into another.

It was a tradition for our youth group to go on retreat every Labor Day weekend, so we could pray and prepare ourselves for the coming school year. It was held in the Florida panhandle, south of Montgomery, Alabama, where we lived. I had turned eighteen the previous autumn and would be leaving for a college just south of Birmingham soon. I wanted one more time to participate, even though I had graduated from high school the previous spring.

Our mornings were spent in listening and discussing and then being sent off to pray. I remember that we were to pray for fifteen minutes, and I had the hardest time "filling" that time up—years later, when I was leading women on retreat, I made sure to give some suggestions and guidance to help those who might find themselves in the same position.

After our spiritual time, all of us young people would head to the beach across the highway, towels across our arms and sandals on our feet. Some of us older girls laid our towels down quite a bit up the beach, toward the sand dunes, to work on our suntans.

A young man named Ed was one of our leaders that year. He was a senior at Columbia Theological Seminary in Decatur, Georgia. And something happened that summer's day on the beach. For the first time, he saw me not as Buddy's kid sister but as a young woman ready for her first year of college. A short time after that, he started coming home more often for weekend visits and spending time with me. We dated quite a lot, and it became a growing attraction for both of us. If we were home on the same weekend, he would call my father up and say he had to go to Montevallo (my college town) on his way back to seminary and would be happy to take me back. Daddy always enjoyed Ed saying things like that, knowing what was behind it.

But by spring, something changed. I knew that after his graduation, Ed was going to serve a church for a year before going to the mission field. I knew he wanted to serve in Brazil and also learned that the mission board stipulated that a missionary's wife should have a college education. By the time Ed would be ready to leave the country, I would have only been in college for two years. The writing was on the wall. Ed and I talked and knew we would have to break off our relationship. It hurt. I finally had met someone who was mature, who wanted to serve God—and now I had to give him up! In the midst of the acute disappointment, though, I sensed God saying something to me: "Yes, Jan, this is someone like the one you have hoped for—but he is not the one." That was the first reminder of faithfulness. Those years were not wasted. God had allowed me to spend that time with Ed so I could have a measuring rod to go by. He was encouraging me with this perspective: The kind of man I wanted to spend my life with was out there, because I had already met one example.

Still, young man after young man came and went. One day, as I walked down the hallway of Johns Hopkins Hospital in Baltimore, just before attending an InterVarsity Christian Fellowship mission meeting, I said to God, "I haven't met anyone yet, but I want to serve you. I don't feel strong enough by myself. But if I don't meet anyone like Ed, then help me to serve you by myself."

Not two hours later, I laid my eyes on my future husband.

Eugene was leading the singing before the missionary talk at the InterVarsity meeting. He had the most beautiful smile—when he smiled, his eyes almost closed up. He was blond, and from my vantage point in the sixth row of this huge teaching amphitheater, I thought his eyes were blue and sparkling. I was enchanted. I only got to shyly say hi to him in the aisle after the meeting (and he was shy too— I found out later that he had noticed me, as well). But, typical of my husband-to-be, he went down to the book table and we didn't get to really meet each other. All the way home, I dreamed of his smile and manner. Would I see him again? Where did he come from? I told one of my friends on the drive home that I was going to start going to InterVarsity meetings again.

I attended a college-and-career young adult group at a neighboring church on Sunday evenings. I had been asked to lead the singing for that next Sunday. Our speaker was a graduate student from South Africa who was to speak to us about apartheid. Charles Fensham didn't know his way around Baltimore, of course, and he asked Eugene, a fellow student, if he would go with him to this meeting. Eugene had planned to go downtown to hear Handel's *Messiah*, but out of Christian duty, he accompanied Charles instead. Was there ever an answer to prayer! When he saw me singing, he was determined to talk with me and learn my name. We did get to talk over refreshments after the program, and I finagled a ride home with the friend who was taking Charles and Eugene back to Hopkins.

Eugene and I sat in the backseat and talked the whole way. I told him that my brother and I were going to the InterVarsity missionary conference in Urbana, Illinois, at the end of the year. While I was at the conference, I received a letter from Eugene! It was quite a letter. He had also sent me a dozen red roses for Christmas, which was very romantic. (He had gone home to Montana for Christmas because he hadn't been home for a year.) I let a girlfriend read the letter, and she said, "A kiss is coming." How did she know?

We were married eight months later.

My marriage to Eugene is just one piece of God's faithfulness over my life, but it is a significant one. When Ed and I broke off our relationship, I could have been discouraged that the "right man" had gotten away. But instead, God helped me see the bigger picture. Looking back at the beginning of my relationship with Eugene, I see such beauty in how God worked. And he has continued to work. He has faithfully encouraged us both in the good times and hard times in our marriage over so many years now.

Even in our winter season, I find such encouragement reflecting on God's faithfulness to us. And now I pass that encouragement on to you: When you are in a season where you can't see what God is doing, know that he is indeed working. He is weaving something in the silence of your days, and you will be able to look back and see what he was creating in the darkness.

OFFERING ENCOURAGEMENT

We all need encouragement throughout our lives. But once we've received it, how do we give that encouragement—in tangible and significant ways—to others on the journey? Sometimes it's easy to see what we can do to help and encourage a friend. Sometimes we need to be quite creative. We don't want to preach, we don't want to be bossy, and we want to encourage in the most loving ways we know how. Sometimes this looks like using intentional words to encourage someone, and sometimes it looks like simply being present and investing in their life.

I met my young friend Sherry during our Regent

College days in Vancouver. I spent quite a bit of time with her, and we developed a rich friendship before she and her husband returned to the States to serve in a church there.

Sherry and I liked each other and enjoyed each other's presence and our conversations. I wanted to do something special for her on leaving and asked her if she would like to go to Bowen Island for a day's retreat. She readily agreed, and we drove to the ferry and took the short ride over to the small island. We walked to a friend's house and put our simple lunches down in her guest cabin next door. I had prearranged this accommodation in case of rain. We walked down the road to a small lake and sat down on a bench. I suggested we go into The Silence for half an hour or so and ask God to prepare our hearts for our time together. Sherry had told me earlier that the one creature in life she didn't like was a snake. As we sat on the bench meditating, a wriggling water snake on the water's surface slithered his way toward us. Sherry and I met each other's eye at the same time and smiled. Does the Lord have a sense of humor?

Later, after we had eaten our lunch, we sat outside on the deck of the cabin and I told Sherry I had written her a letter that I would like to read aloud to her. I had enjoyed encouraging her through our friendship and our time together, but now was the time to encourage her in specific and intentional words.

Dear Sherry,

These last two years at Regent have been a door into a new room for you, haven't they? Jesus tells us he has rooms prepared for us in heaven, which is a wonderful promise to us as Christians. But to be ready to enter, to be received, into those *rooms, we have some of our own "rooms" to enter here on earth so that we* can *enter those in the heavenly places. In C. S. Lewis's book* The Great Divorce, *the people who have never spent time with God or known much about him find that the grass in heaven is sharp and impossible to walk on, that it hurts their feet terribly. On the other hand, the ones who have walked in God's country on earth find the grass soft and welcoming to their feet*

*(and souls). They're "at home" with this country.
It seems this is what our journey here on earth is
about—to walk in God's country.*

*Sherry, I believe these past several months of
conversation with each other have been part of
getting better acquainted with God's country,
and I rejoice in what this has meant for both
of us.*

*This country is endless in its adventures.
There is always new territory to peek at and
enter into. Some new valley with lovely lakes to
sit beside and find rest in our souls; some new
mountain peak to scale and feel satisfaction and
joy in doing something hard that we didn't think
we could do; some alpine meadow with its vast
array of color, shape, and texture in all the little
wild flowers that bring delight and joy to our eyes
and souls. This is God's country with its rest and
renewal, its hardships and challenges and with
its profusion of delights—and all of this custom-
made for us as Sherry and as Jan, as Tom and as
Eugene, Karen, Stephen, Eric, Anna, Leif, Sarah*

[our husbands and children]. *Each of us is an original.*

How do I see you, Sherry? A woman a lot like me who finds joy in serving others, a doer, a Dorcas, someone who not only serves and gets the job done but also gives herself away to others while doing the serving. Being a Martha, if you will.

But now at this time in your life, just *being a Martha is not enough anymore. And* this *is the new room of your life you are being beckoned to enter, I believe. To walk through that door (is it the kitchen door?) into the living room and sit at the feet of Jesus and be a Mary.*

I think once we sit at the feet of Jesus, carve out those quiet moments of looking lovingly into his face, that that devotion and quiet spirit will follow us back into the place of serving— but now, having more of him within us, our serving will be expanded in a subliminal way. Something more is happening as we do those things daily life requires of us. Many of the saints were extremely active, busy people dealing with people of the world, not shut off and cloistered.

Sitting at Jesus' feet and then returning to serve is kind of like setting aside yourself and watching what God is going to do next in your life and in those around you as you serve. We're not manipulating and making things happen. We're simply providing the space, the hospitality to let God do something. He invites us to participate with him. And to me, it is so joyful when I have these moments of awareness that he is present and doing something so much bigger than Jan Peterson.

You've entered that room already, Sherry, maybe a little falteringly, maybe bumping into the furniture or tripping over a left-behind shoe, but keeping your eye on that footstool to go and sit at his feet. He sits there ready for us, always loving and accepting us.

As you feel more at home in the living room, you'll come to love that footstool more and more. You'll always serve—that's a big part of who you are—but you'll be serving with an added dimension to your life. And it sums up to equal joy.

I don't quite know how to end this letter, Sherry, except to say "thank you" to both you and God for this privilege of being fellow journeyers in this God-country.

Fondly,
Jan

And so do you see how encouragement pulls together all of the things we've talked about in the rest of this book? Friendship is giving and receiving. It is serving and caring and allowing ourselves to be served and cared for. At the end of the day, encouragement is what helps us see ourselves and our lives more clearly. It helps us reorient ourselves to what we may be missing as we reach out in friendship and what we may need to receive from the Lord and others in order to offer the most whole and healthy versions of ourselves to others. A spiritual friend calls out the good things in us and encourages us when we stumble. *This way, this way.* She points us to what God is doing and what he may want to do in us.

Are you weary and lonely? Do you long for greater connection with the Lord and with others? May you find a compassionate spiritual friend to walk alongside you and encourage you.

Encouragement

1. Who is the most encouraging person you know?
   What makes them encouraging?

2. What do you need most in your life right now—
   support, confidence, or hope? Who can you turn to
   for this kind of encouragement?

3. Did you grow up seeing encouragement modeled well? If so, how did that develop your ability to encourage others? If not, how do you choose to develop a rhythm of encouragement?

4. Reflect back on a season of God's faithfulness. What do you understand now that you didn't at the time? How does this reflection encourage you for the future?

5. Who in your life needs encouragement? What encouraging words or actions will be most meaningful to this friend?

EPILOGUE

$\mathcal{H}$ERE WE ARE at the end of our journey today, but at the beginning of your journey into deeper and more spiritually meaningful friendships. I hope and pray that these words have encouraged you to take a risk or two to develop faithful friendships that will impact not only your life but also those of your friends.

To be encouraged and to encourage in relationships

can make such a difference in our lives. I know it has for me. For example, I felt I was a better pastor's wife to the women in our congregation when Clare and I were meeting and encouraging each other in our journeys. I could give myself to them because I was being nourished in a faithful friendship that was helping to meet some of my needs.[12]

Whenever I am surrounded by faithful friends, I don't feel so isolated (as many of us do in this busy world of ours). When we don't feel so alone, we have the energy to reach out to others.

Perhaps the person you're drawn to reach out to is hurting or just needs to be welcomed into the community. You're not being drained of energy that you hardly have, because with a faithful friend, you yourself are getting benefits that help to energize you.

If you are a pastor's wife, may I offer a bit of advice? I never felt I could or should develop an intimate friendship within the church as the pastor's wife. (I did have a good friend in the church, but I wasn't as free with her as I was with my friends from outside the church.) I didn't want anyone's feelings to get hurt. Of course, there are going to be some women you will like and enjoy being with in the church, but I still think you have to be mindful that you don't hurt anyone's feelings so that they feel left out. The church is not a club. We are to love and care for the entire body of believers, so I felt having a close friend from our congregation was probably not very wise. So if you are a pastor's wife, I would suggest that you find someone outside your church, a person who is a member of another church in your community or outside your neighborhood, who has a personal walk with Jesus and would be a good "soul friend."

No matter where you are in life, as you engage in a friendship that builds you up in your journey, I hope that the five elements that we have talked about in this little book—caring, accepting, serving, offering hospitality, and encouraging—may ring a bell in your own soul and help guide you. And I pray that you will be able to find another woman who can engage with you in each of these areas, someone who can be that "faithful friend" with and for you.

Know this: Your deepening friendship doesn't

have to be structured and detailed. When I look back on my early friendship with Clare, I remember how we worked the details out as we went along. The specific form and outworking of your spiritual friendship will come as you get acquainted and start sharing your inner selves with each other. Our God is a faithful God. He is with us and in us, even in our friendships. Perhaps especially in our friendships—for he is also a profoundly relational God.

FINAL REFLECTIONS

Reflect on what you've learned on this journey of spiritual friendship. How will you change your approach to your friendships? Who will you invest in? Who will you seek out to invest in you?

AFTERWORD

by Eugene Peterson

EVERYONE IS IN A process of becoming. More gradually than rapidly, we grow into the unique people we were created to be, through a lifetime of learning Christ and practicing the way of Jesus. We aren't given a lot of time; threescore and ten, or fourscore if we're lucky, according to the psalmist.[13] But eighty years is still a relatively short time to prepare for citizenship in the Kingdom of God. With everybody a rookie in the process of growing up in Christ, we need all the help we can get. We especially need the help of one another.

Fortunately, we were designed to be in relationship

with others. For all of the goodness that erupts from the pages of the Creation accounts, the one thing that gets described otherwise is aloneness: "It's not good for the Man to be alone; I'll make him a helper, a companion" (Genesis 2:18). What was true for Adam has been true for every daughter and son of Adam since the beginning of humanity. We need the companionship of fellow disciples as we make the lifelong pilgrimage from infancy to adulthood, and then, paradoxically, back to learning how to become like children again. Such companions, whether in the form of spouses or friends, have holy agency: Our lives are healed and shaped by the people whose company we keep. Now, well into our octogenarian years, Jan and I are still in that process of becoming, having not yet arrived, although we are beginning to glimpse—even to lean toward—the finish line.

I remember fondly the season in our lives when Jan and I took a full year's sabbatical from our pastoral assignment. At the end of each month we would send a two-sided letter from our lake house in Montana to our church home in Maryland as a way of staying in communication with our congregation. "Gene's side" was full of the ideas I was working into the three books I managed to complete that year. "Jan's side" gave updates on our children and grandchildren. It included reports of the guests we hosted, and the birds and wild flowers we identified through the four seasons. It always concluded with what we were having for dinner that particular evening. Little was my surprise to hear that people invariably preferred the more personal side that Jan wrote.

I have always occupied the world of ideas and have enjoyed nurturing a life of the mind. Jan's calling, in blessed contrast, has ushered her into the rich world of people, where she has devoted her life to the sacred task of offering hospitality, creating safe spaces for others to become themselves. Because of her uncommon knack for connecting with people, even our daily trips to the post office these days take an inordinate amount of time because Jan knows nearly everybody in town, and always takes time to give them some of her signature attention. To do otherwise would be to dishonor her image-of-God self.

From raising our children, to caring for parishioners, to attending guests, and enjoying the mutuality of her many friendships, Jan has incarnated the life of Christ by being present to others. In that lifelong process, not only has she become more and more like her old friend Gertrude, she has become more like her Savior.

Over the years I have delighted in the woman Jan has become, as she has immersed herself in a wide and deep variety of relationships. During our sixty-year marriage covenant, we have been fellow bond servants, partners in life and in ministry. While I have written extensively on spiritual theology, she has practiced the art of spiritual friendship, "always present, always caring." She is the most practical theologian I know. Through the deeply personal friendships she has invested herself in over the course of a lifetime, she has become more her God-created self in the company of others.

As I have in hers.

Eugene H. Peterson
Lakeside, MT
Easter Sunday, 2018

Acknowledgments

$\mathcal{I}$ WISH TO THANK Esther Brinkley, who moved to Montana after retiring from the publication department at Fuller Seminary and encouraged me to write my story. After I read some of the early pieces of this book to Esther, she said to me, "I knew you had a story in you." She has been a great encourager.

I also wish to thank my friend Don Pape, the publisher at NavPress, who urged me on to write my story and helped me get started. He showed me that "it's never too late in your life to do something new." Here I am at almost eighty-three years of age, and I have written my first book!

And my acquisitions editor at NavPress, Caitlyn Carlson—I am indebted to her for guiding me along in the writing. She was a very warm and encouraging friend as well. Thank you, Caitlyn, for treating me with such grace and gentleness.

And I also wish to thank my copy editor, Elizabeth Symm, who, though it was a brief time working together, brought the full circle of writing, editing, and getting it printed completed.

Thank you to friends and family members who knew about the book, for asking me from time to time how it was coming along—that served as encouragement to me. Thank you Eric, Leif, Karen; sisters-in-law Polly and Karen; my tai chi friends; and many other friends who knew this was a new venture for me.

And, of course, I wish to thank my loving and devoted husband of sixty years, to whom I have dedicated this book, for his encouraging word here and there. Thank you, Eugene, for standing alongside me—and for patience in sometimes waiting for your lunch or supper.

Notes

1. Dorothy Day, *The Long Loneliness: The Autobiography of the Legendary Catholic School Activist* (San Francisco, CA: HarperSanFrancisco, 1997), 285–86.
2. Luke 6:31, NIV
3. 1 John 4:7, RSV
4. Wendell Berry, *Leavings: Poems* (Berkeley, CA: Counterpoint, 2010), 40.
5. Henri J. M. Nouwen, *Reaching Out: The Three Movements of the Spiritual Life* (New York: Image Books, 2013), 65.
6. Nouwen, *Reaching Out*, 70.
7. See Aaron Raverty, OSB, "Hospitality in the Benedictine Monastic Tradition," *REMHU: Revista Interdisciplinar da Mobildade Humana* 20, no. 38 (January/June 2012): 251–55, accessed February 13, 2018, https://digitalcommons.csbsju.edu/cgi/.cgi?article=1003 &context=saint_johns_abbey_pubs. For the account of Abraham welcoming the three strangers, see Genesis 18:1-15.
8. Partially paraphrased; see Luke 10:25-37, NIV.
9. This book was recently reprinted. See David Dunn, *Try Giving Yourself Away* (Andesite Press, 2017).

10. Albert Borgmann, *Technology and the Character of Contemporary Life: A Philosophical Inquiry* (Chicago: University of Chicago Press, 1984), 4.

11. David Riesman, Nathan Glazer, and Reuel Denney, *The Lonely Crowd: A Study on the Changing American Character* (New Haven, CT: Yale University Press, 1961, 1989).

12. If you are looking for another resource to encourage you on your friendship journey, I'd recommend an old little booklet called *Faithful Friendship* by Dorothy Devers. Clare and I found reading and talking about it immensely helpful as we started out in our friendship. It is out of print after all these years, but you can find it available used online!

13. See Psalm 90:10, RSV.